MANGA CROSS-STITCH

> MAKE YOUR OWN GRAPHIC ART NEEDLEWORK

Helen McCarthy

MANGA CROSS-STITCH

> MAKE YOUR OWN
GRAPHIC ART NEEDLEWORK

Designs by Steve Kyte and Helen McCarthy

For information, write to:
Andrews McMeel Publishing, LLC,
an Andrews McMeel Universal company,
1130 Walnut Street,
Kansas City,
Missouri 64106

09 10 11 12 13 CTP 10 9 8 7 6 5 4 3 2 1

ISBN-13: 978-0-7407-7965-7
ISBN-10: 0-7407-7965-6
Library of Congress Control Number: 2009922825
www.andrewsmcmeel.com

This book was conceived, designed,
and produced by
THE ILEX PRESS LIMITED
210 High Street, Lewes, BN7 2NS, UK

ILEX Editorial, Lewes:
Publisher: Alastair Campbell
Creative Director: Peter Bridgewater
Managing Editor: Nick Jones
Editor: Ellie Wilson
Commissioning Editor: Tim Pilcher
Art Director: Julie Weir
Designers: Chris and Jane Lanaway
Art Editor: Emily Harbison

CONTENTS

Chapter 1

MATERIALS AND TECHNIQUES

Chapter 2

DESIGN YOUR OWN STITCHED MANGA PAGES

Chapter 3
CUTE CREATURES AND CHARACTERS

Chapter 4
ACTION AND ADVENTURE

Chapter 5
SCREENTONE AND VISUAL EFFECTS

Chapter 6
LETTERING

MANGA, ANIME, AND STITCHES
> INTRODUCTION

MANGA AND ANIME (Japanese for comics and animation) are big news—and big business—all over the world. Japan's contemporary visual culture influences artists and designers in fields from video, film, and music to packaging and robotics. The energy and diversity of styles make it a gold mine for anyone involved with creating images and telling stories.

Creative, relaxing, and beautiful, embroidery can easily fit alongside other activities—chatting, traveling, listening to music, watching TV. It can be as original and challenging as you choose, yet it unwinds life's tensions. Your time and effort yield lasting, beautiful results.

Anime and manga offer a new way to look at stitching. Printed or digital images are made by arranging blocks of color. Counted-thread embroidery does the same. Outline work is common to both graphics and stitching. Even screentones used in Japanese comics echo the patterns in blackwork embroidery.

There's a huge amount of talent and enthusiasm for both arts, but not much overlap between the two. This book attempts to bridge the gap, to encourage artists to use the ancient skills of embroidery to make anime and manga images, and to urge stitchers to tap into a whole new visual grammar.

If you're new to counted-thread work, you might want to start with one or two simple manga-style panels—single figures on a plain background, using Aida cloth and one color. Experienced embroiderers who are new to manga and anime might try one of the color splash-page charts, or a large black and white image, using stitching to replicate screentones. Fans who already stitch will probably want to dive in and assemble their own mega-project.

You can scan pictures and stitch them using some of the ideas and techniques in this book, or follow the charts provided. You may also want to start creating your own unique stitched images. Make something original. Let your inner artist have some fun!

The book is arranged so that you can learn basic counted-thread stitches, find the materials and equipment you need, and build up

a design from basic layout to finishing touches. The CD gives you all the charts and patterns, plus some helpful extras like a demo version of the software used for viewing and creating these manga designs.

This book comes from a collision of old and new art forms. Where it goes from here is up to you. Enjoy the journey from ancient craft to 21st-century art form.

Manga style can be expressed through cross-stitch techniques for a fresh perspective.

Images by Yishan Li

MANGA, ANIME, AND STITCHES
> A SHORT HISTORY

The word *manga* (usually translated as "inconsequential" or "irresponsible" pictures) was brought to prominence by Japanese artist Katsushika Hokusai. Fifteen volumes of his sketches appeared under the title *Hokusai Manga*, starting in 1814. Japan already had a long tradition of humorous or scandalous drawings, used to teach, preach, and entertain. During the 18th century, the rise of a wealthy urban middle class, visually literate and style-conscious, led to massive sales of woodblock prints.

The influx of Western ideas and publications in the 19th century inspired Japanese publishers to create comic strips and satirical magazines. The modern manga industry began in 1946, when teenager Osamu Tezuka published his first professional comic. Tezuka used cinematic techniques to tell stories in a new way, and his success revolutionized Japanese comics. In modern Japan, manga are a popular form of entertainment for people of all ages and interests.

Japanese artists began making animated movies in the early 20th century. When television came to Japan, Osamu Tezuka was among the first to see its potential for anime. His pioneering science fiction series *Tetsuwan Atom* was screened in 1961. Later that year, Americans saw it under the title *Astro Boy*.

A waterfall by Katsushika Hokusai, who popularized the word *manga* through his free, irreverent sketches of everyday life.

At the end of the 20th century "Cool Japan," the home of cutting-edge technology, comics, and animation, became a worldwide youth cult. For the first time, anime and manga made big inroads into public consciousness in the English-speaking world.

Decorative needlework has been around since people first made clothes. Many ancient civilizations valued embroidery, including Egypt and China. In Europe, the oldest surviving embroideries date from the Middle Ages. One famous narrative embroidery, the Bayeux Tapestry, is a record of William the Conqueror's invasion of England in 1066, laid out almost like a Japanese narrative scroll—or a comic strip.

Many early embroiderers and designers were men. They set up trade guilds to regulate training and working conditions all over Europe. Women also embroidered, both as paid employees and at home for their families. By the time Swiss immigrant Jacob Schiess set up the first modern embroidery workshop, in New York in 1848, men could earn more in heavy industry, and stitching was mainly a woman's job.

The first embroidery machines were created in Switzerland in the 1860s, making mass production possible. Most commercial embroidery now is mass produced by machine. Very few people can afford the exquisite hand embroidery that is a hallmark of haute couture clothing or home décor—unless they learn to do it themselves. With developments in sewing technology, both hand and machine embroidery can be created to professional standards at home.

As a stitcher, you are part of a long tradition of artists and crafters who have used their skills to beautify everyday life. Inspired by your own interests and ideas, you can create images based on manga, using a contemporary art form in harmony with one of the most ancient crafts.

Manga are usually printed in black and white, or monotone. The black outline is crucial to the style of manga and anime artwork.

HOW TO USE THE CD
> THE BASICS

THE SOFTWARE ON this CD will enable you to print out all the charts in the book, in several different formats, as often as you want. It will also enable you to personalize your projects by changing the colors of the stitches. The full program, available from Ursa Software at a discounted price for readers, will enable you to design new charts of your own, which you can do using elements in the charts provided with this package, as well as your own motifs.

The CD contains the Project Index, so you can look up charts quickly—the charts are listed by chapter and in the order that they appear in the book.

TO LOAD THE PROGRAM ONTO YOUR MAC

1. Insert the disc into your computer and double-click on the CD icon when it appears on your desktop.
2. Read the license agreement. You must agree to the terms to use the Manga Cross-Stitch package.
3. Double-click on the Step 2 icon to begin installing the MacStitch program and follow the on-screen instructions.
4. Once installed, the program should be saved to your Applications folder, within the MacStitch Pattern Viewer (Manga) folder, where you will also find the Manga Charts folder containing the designs in this book. For quick access to these charts, you can copy them directly to your desktop, or somewhere equally convenient, by dragging

the Extras: Manga Charts icon onto your desktop. You can also do this for the Project Index, which is where you will find detailed information and the requirements for each project in this book.

TO LOAD THE PROGRAM ONTO YOUR PC

1. Insert the disc into your computer.
2. Read the license agreement. You must agree to the terms to use the Manga Cross-Stitch package.
3. Click on installer, and follow the on-screen instructions, as it tells you to chose Install, and then Finish. Please be patient while it copies the program onto your destop. Once it has done so, the Stitch icon will appear. For quick access to the Project Index, you can copy it onto your desktop, or somewhere equally convenient.

MAKING CROSS-STITCH CHARTS
ON YOUR COMPUTER

Counted-thread embroiderers reproduce designs on fabric by counting regular threads or blocks to put stitches of the same size in the right place. A cross-stitch chart is a diagram that shows you exactly where to put each stitch so that the picture you end up with is the same as the one on your chart.

Every square on a chart represents a single cross-stitch. A square divided diagonally represents a fractional stitch or stitches. Backstitch is represented by a line. If you lose your place, you can count the stitches you've completed to find where the next one needs to go.

When you open the MacStitch or Stitch program, you will see what looks like a sheet of graph paper on your screen. This is a blank chart. Using simple point-and-click or dialog-based operations, you can put your own design onto it. (However, you will need the full version of the program to be able to print or save this design.)

You make your design using a mouse or trackpad to add one of the stitches on the toolbar onscreen to a square on the chart. The stitch you choose appears in the color highlighted on the palette at the bottom of the chart. Undoing mistakes is easy, so, with a little practice, even complete beginners can design and print their own charts.

The onscreen toolbar has a list of dialogs, each with a range of functions. The final one, About, contains details of the program and the Help file. New stitchers and designers who haven't used the program before should read the Help file first to find out what it can do.

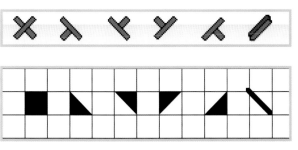

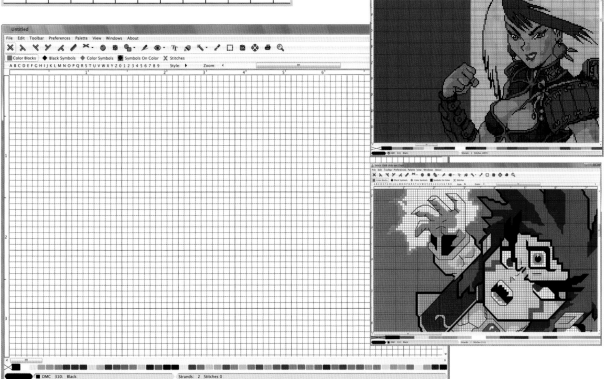

HOW TO USE THE CD
> PREPARING TO STITCH

PRINTING YOUR CHARTS

The program will display and print out charts in color blocks, black symbols on white, colored symbols, black symbols on color blocks, or cross-stitches. So you can choose the format you want to design in and the format you prefer to work from.

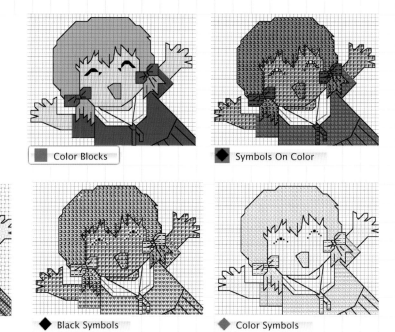

■ Color Blocks

◆ Symbols On Color

✗ Stitches

◆ Black Symbols

◆ Color Symbols

I find it easiest to design and stitch with color blocks, but many stitchers find black symbols on white or color easier to work from. If the light or your printout is not very good, it can be hard to tell what color is on the chart.

Before you print a symbol chart, the program allows you to edit your threads and symbols, using Edit Current Thread in the Palette menu. When the computer selects symbols, it sometimes uses the same one twice, or puts two similar symbols together. By editing the symbols you can eliminate duplicates and choose ones that are easier to see.

Print your chart at a size you can read easily. The program gives you the option of printing it at any size between four and 40 blocks to the inch. At four blocks to the inch your chart will be very large, using lots of paper and ink, and at 40 blocks to the inch no ordinary human could follow it. Usually, if you have lots of color changes over a small area, a bigger chart will be easier to follow. Printing at eight blocks to the inch is a compromise between economy and legibility that works for most stitchers.

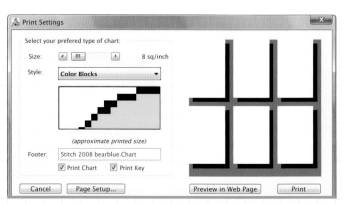

BUYING STRANDED COTTON/FLOSS

The program works out how many inches of each stranded cotton shade your design will use. When you're ready to print your chart, you also get a key that shows you how much of each color you need.

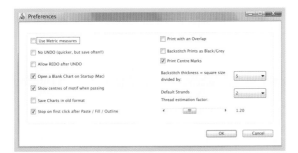

Everyone works differently, so if you find you regularly run short of thread or have lots left over, you can adjust the Thread Estimation Factor in the Preferences dialog box and the program will alter the amount of thread listed in the key from then on.

A standard DMC skein of six-stranded cotton is 8 meters, or 8.75 yards/315 inches, long. If you're stitching in two threads, this means you'll get 945 inches of thread in a skein. Allowing for average tension, unpicking, and thread to fasten on and off, it's assumed that each skein will make about 2,100 stitches. Dividing the number of stitches in the color key by 2,100 tells you how many skeins of each color you need.

Some retailers sell half skeins or quarter skeins, which is helpful if you only need a small amount of one color and think you won't use it again.

PREPARING TO WORK

The program marks the center of your chart. Marking the center of your fabric will help you to keep the design on track and put each stitch in the right place.

You can do this by folding the fabric in quarters and marking the center with a pin, or by stitching (in a contrast color) in a straight line along the folds. The center is where the stitched lines cross. Unpick your guidelines when you no longer need them—you can leave them in until you've finished, if you like.

Many stitchers start at the center, but you can start anywhere: Starting at the top or bottom, or in one corner, is fine. Some people like to finish all stitches in one color at a time, starting from the darkest and working through to the lightest. Some prefer to stitch the outlines first, others to get the largest areas of color done and then work to the smallest, and some like to stitch a whole line at a time. For the best definition, finish your cross-stitches first, and then add any backstitch on top.

MATERIALS AND TECHNIQUES

BASIC MATERIALS
> EQUIPMENT AND FABRICS

YOU DON'T NEED much to start counted-thread embroidery —needles, small scissors, fabric and thread, and a waterproof bag or box to keep your work and materials clean and dry in between stitching sessions.

Always buy the best quality equipment you can afford. Good materials are easier to use, look better, and last longer. You can order materials online if there's no craft shop in your area.

Needles for cross-stitch have blunt ends, so as not to split the individual threads, and large eyes. The surface of the metal roughens with use—you should ideally use a new needle for each large project. Gold-plated needles are more expensive but stitch more smoothly. For the projects in this book, a size 24 or 26 needle is a good choice.

Small, pointed scissors with narrow blades cut thread neatly and help you to unpick mistakes and tidy up your work. Keep them dry and sharp, and never use them for cutting paper or fabric.

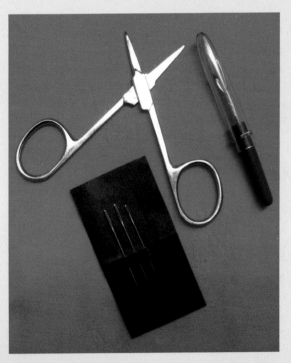

Gold-plated needles make stitching easier, while scissors and seam rippers help to unpick any mistakes.

FABRICS

Counted-thread embroidery is done on evenweave fabric, with an even number of threads per inch. Many suppliers offer advice on choosing the right fabric for your project, which is vital for manga-style pieces.

Aida is made up of threads woven in square blocks with holes at each corner. Every stitch is worked over one square. Most stitchers start out working on Aida, or the larger version Binca, and many are happy to stay with it.

Cotton and cotton-mix fabrics vary in stiffness and sheen as well as color, offering a range of effects. Smooth, slightly shiny cloth like Jobelan gives the impression of high-quality paper, while slightly uneven fabric like Quaker Cloth simulates coarser paper.

Linen has many brand names. Most linen has a slub, or variation, in the thread. This can give your work the roughness of a manga anthology, or the elegance of handmade paper.

You can embroider on non-evenweave fabrics, like knits or PVC, with easy-to-use waste canvas, a stiff evenweave bound with glue. Tack it onto your chosen fabric, and stitch the design over it. Be careful not to stitch through any of the canvas threads. Dampen the area and gently pull each thread out, leaving your design on the fabric.

When buying fabric, always allow at least three inches extra on all four sides for handling and framing. For an image that measures 10 by 12 inches, you will need a piece of fabric at least 16 by 18 inches. It's a good idea to overcast or hem the raw edges so they won't fray while you're working.

BASIC MATERIALS
> THREAD COUNTS AND SIZING

THREAD COUNTS

Thread count—the number of threads per inch in a fabric—can also be described as holes per inch, or HPI. Aida is described as "14 HPI" or "14 count." Evenweaves have 28, 36, or even more holes per inch. These are usually "stitched over two"—each stitch covers a block of two threads in both directions.

SIZING

Most designs in this book have been test-stitched on fabric with 14 holes, or 28 threads per inch. Using a higher HPI makes a smaller finished piece: the lower the HPI, the larger the finished piece.

To work out how big a finished design is going to be, divide the number of stitches along each side of the design by the HPI. That gives you the length in inches.

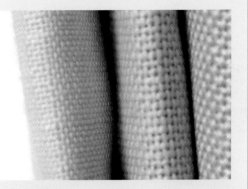

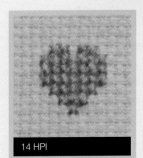

14 HPI

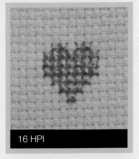

16 HPI

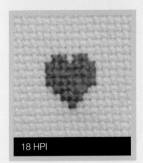

18 HPI

The higher the HPI count is, the smaller the finished work will be. For example, a design measuring 35 stitches wide by 56 stitches long on 14 HPI would be 2.5 × 4 inches. Stitched on 16 HPI, it would be 2.19 × 3.5 inches, and on 20 HPI, 1.75 × 2.8 inches.

RESIZING MOTIFS

If you're assembling motifs into a new design, you can change the sizes using a photocopier, or scan them into a computer and resize to fit your project. You can also scan in motifs from any copyright-free source to create backgrounds or figures, again resized to fit your design.

You can print or copy motifs at various sizes and arrange them on paper the size of the finished piece, until the arrangement looks right. You can also do this on a computer. This helps to make sure the project is the right size and everything fits together.

When you resize motifs, you need to ensure they are all stitched at the same HPI by laying a new graph over the design. You can buy tracing paper with scaled grids or transparent acetate graph paper to fix over your design. It's more expensive than tracing paper, but reusable.

Screen graph programs overlay a graph on your computer, turning any image into an instant chart. There's one on the CD with this book. Most cross-stitch charting programs will also turn the images you import into charts.

OTHER MATERIALS
> THREADS, BEADS, AND MORE

THREADS

Stranded cotton, or floss, is sold in six-strand skeins. Using one strand to make your stitches gives a fine line but won't cover the fabric well. Four strands give dense coverage but are hard to pull through the fabric.

The designs in this book use two threads of stranded cotton in one color. Try out other types of thread for different effects. Different threads and strands create contrast.

A blending filament—a clear or colored polymer strand—mixed with your thread will create the effect of rain or dew, or add subtle highlights. On this cute cat's face, a pearlized thread highlights the sun marking on his forehead and complements the gleaming thread woven into the fabric background. Glitter, fluorescent, or ultraviolet threads give stronger effects.

This chart is approximately 54 stitches wide by 45 stitches tall. At 14 HPI it will measure about 3.9 × 3.2 inches (99 × 81 mm).

Piece stitched by Nikki Thompson

EMBELLISHMENTS

Beads and charms heighten texture, while sequins add sparkle. Beads can also be used as highlights for eyes. Lay them on the finished piece to check the effect, and secure them with small stitches in a color that matches the bead or the surrounding area.

Lace, ribbons, and flowers enhance cute or romantic projects. Stitch them to the finished design, or use them to decorate its mounting board. This bunny is embellished with sequins and patches stitched onto the fabric. You can also use printed art as a mount or surround for your stitching.

This chart is approximately 65 stitches wide by 134 stitches tall. At 14 HPI it will measure about 4.6 × 9.6 inches (117 × 244 mm).

Piece stitched by Helen Vale

OTHER EQUIPMENT

Embroidery frames or hoops keep your project stable while you're stitching. I don't use them for small projects, but they're really helpful in keeping an even stitch tension on larger items. A seam ripper is a tiny blade that slides under individual threads to help in unpicking. Lying a dark cloth across your knees or work table makes it easier to see the holes in light fabric. Some threads tangle easily, and running them gently across a block of beeswax or thread conditioner can help prevent this from happening. Over time, you'll build up a collection of equipment that works for you.

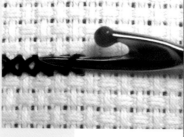

A seam ripper helps you unpick stitches without causing damage to the fabric.

Enhance your stitched images with sew-on charms, like this stone Buddha or these little silver butterflies.

BASIC STITCHES
> CROSS-STITCH

BEFORE YOU START, get a skein of stranded cotton and look at both ends above the paper bands. You'll find the end of a strand where pulling brings cotton out of the skein without unraveling or knotting it.

You can wind your stranded cotton onto a bobbin, but if you leave it in its skein it's already labeled, there's nothing extra to buy, and you can start stitching right away.

To secure the thread, you can start with a loop or with a waste knot. For either method, pull out a six-strand piece of thread around 18 to 20 inches long, and cut it off the skein. (Long strands get worn as you work—shortish is better.) Separate one strand from this piece, then another when you finish the first, and so on.

LOOP

Fold your strand of cotton in half. Thread the cut ends—or the folded end if you find it easier—through the eye of your needle. Pull the folded end down until the needle is about two-thirds to three-quarters of the way along from that end. Each stitch will contain two strands of cotton.

Take your fabric and push the needle through a hole from the back. Take care not to pull the strand all the way through; you want the loop to stay on the back of the fabric. Now push the needle back down diagonally opposite the place it came out, one block (or Aida square, or two threads) away. Push it through the loop, and pull until the stitch is firm but not tight. It shouldn't distort the fabric. Take the needle up through the cloth again, level with where it first came out, but one block away, and down again in the diagonally opposite hole, level with the bottom of your first stitch. You've secured your thread, and made a complete cross-stitch.

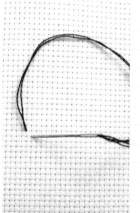 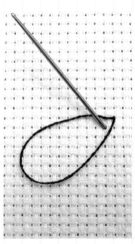 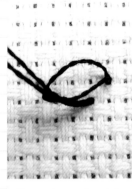

The needle goes through the loop on the back.

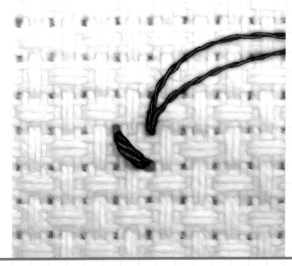

Making the loop creates the first part of the cross-stitch.

WASTE KNOT

Thread your strand through the eye of your needle, until the needle is halfway, and knot the ends. Push the needle through from the front, about ¾ inch in from where you want to start stitching. Bring it back to where you want to start, so that a piece of thread lies on the back of the fabric between the knot and your first stitch.

Take the needle diagonally across one block and through to the back of the fabric. Bring it up through the fabric again, level with where it first came through, but one block away, and down again in the diagonally opposite hole, level with the bottom of your first stitch.

Bring the needle up to the front of the fabric, level with the top of your first stitch, but one block away. Make sure the thread on the back of the fabric is caught under your new stitches.

Keep stitching over the thread until you get to the knot; then snip it off carefully.

FINISHING OFF

Before you run out of thread, take your needle to the back of the cloth and push it under the backs of four or five nearby stitches. Snip off the thread close to the stitching.

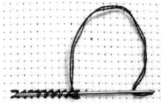

Run your thread back under several completed stitches to secure the end.

CROSS-STITCH IMPERATIVES

Keep your stitch tension even. Pulling too tightly distorts the fabric, wears the thread thin, and changes the shape of the motif.

Make sure that the top part of each stitch goes in the same direction to give a neat surface.

Every few stitches, let the needle and thread hang from the back of the fabric and untwist, so as to avoid uneven stitches.

When possible, bring your needle up from the back, and take it down from the front. This avoids dragging thread ends onto the surface of the design.

1. Ready to start stitching.

2. Making the first cross-stitch.

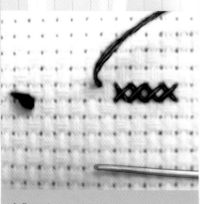

3. Front view.

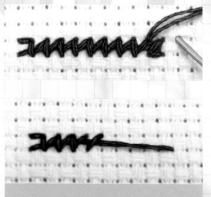

4. Back view—thread caught under stitches.

5. Cut the knot away once your thread is secured.

BASIC STITCHES
> FRACTIONALS, BACKSTITCH, FRENCH KNOTS, AND SEED STITCH

FRACTIONAL STITCHES

Fractional stitches are easier on evenweave, but they can also be worked on Aida, as shown here.

- Half cross-stitch—bring your thread up from the back of the cloth, and take it down, diagonally, one block away.

- Three-quarter cross-stitch—make a half cross. Bring the thread up again at the empty upper or lower corner of the block, depending which way you want the stitch to lie. Bring it down into the middle of the block, or the center hole between the threads. You can cross the first stitch or not, whatever suits the location best.

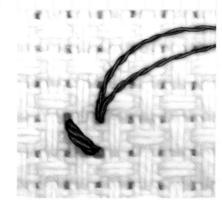

Make a half cross-stitch.

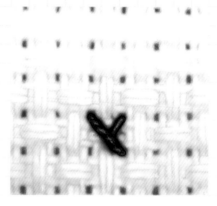

Add a quarter stitch to give a three-quarter cross-stitch.

- Quarter cross-stitch—bring the thread up at one corner of the block, then down in the middle. This fills the gap left by a half cross-stitch.

BACKSTITCH

This outline stitch is worked over one block of Aida or two threads of evenweave. Bring the thread up to the front, then take it down to the back, one block to the right. Bring it up behind the next block to the right, and down again the same distance to the left, joining the first stitch you made. Carry on this way, bringing the needle up to the right of the last stitch, and taking it down to the left into the same hole as the last stitch.

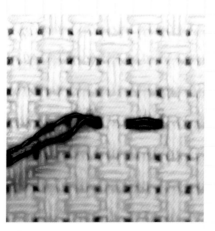

Start with a single straight stitch.

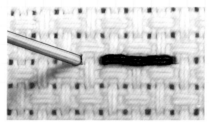

Carry on going under one block/two threads, then back over the same threads.

DOUBLE RUNNING STITCH, HOLBEIN STITCH, OR SPANISH STITCH

This stitch came from Spain with Catherine of Aragon, Henry VIII's first queen. It gives a smooth line. Bring the needle up, down one block away, and so on, working a line of running stitches with one block between each. At the end of the line, go backward, filling the gaps.

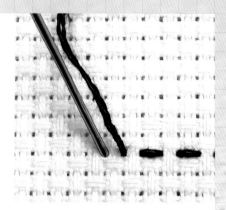

Make a line of even running stitches.

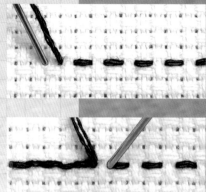

Go back along the line, filling the gaps.

FRENCH KNOT

Bring your needle up where the knot is required. Now twist the needle around the thread twice, and tighten. Slip the point of the needle into the fabric one thread away. Gently pull the needle down through the knot.

The knot is complete once it lies neatly on the surface and the excess thread has gone to the back of the cloth. Keep pulling and the whole stitch will disappear.

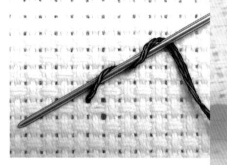

Twist the needle around the thread twice.

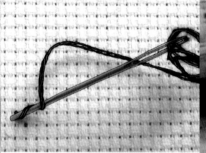

Keeping the twists tight, take the needle down through them and the fabric.

SEED STITCH

This is a useful little stitch for shading or filling blank areas. Don't use a dark thread on a light background unless you want it to show through the cloth. Take a straight stitch of one block or half a block in any direction, and continue as necessary.

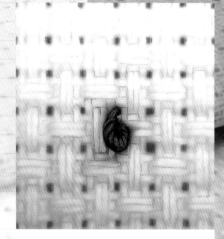

The finished knot.

COMPLEX STITCHES
> ADDING TEXTURE AND DEPTH

MANGA USES PATTERN and density to create shapes and add surface interest. You can do this in the same way, using black line stitching, but there are lots of interesting stitches that add texture and form. Here are just a few, plus a very simple chart (page 29) to help you practice. If you want to try more, have a look at some stitching books or Internet sites.

BRICK STITCH

Single rows of stitches worked in a zigzag form a tiny diamond pattern, or distinct zigzags if worked in different colors. Work over one or two threads of evenweave. On Aida, work with four strands or a thick, heavy thread for better coverage.

Bring the needle up from the back of the cloth, then down two blocks above. Bring it up again one block to the left, level with the middle of the last stitch. Take it down two blocks below. Bring it up again one block to the left and level

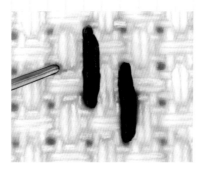

Stitches offset like bricks give the stitch its name.

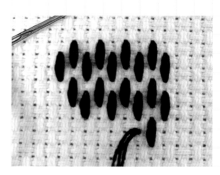

The rows of stitches should interlock.

with the top of your first stitch. Take it down two blocks below, level with the bottom of your first stitch. Continue like

this to the end of the row, then work back, fitting your new stitches into the base of the previous row.

TENT STITCH

This alternative to cross-stitch is like a line of half crosses, but the long slanting stitches on the back make it hardwearing and give good coverage on evenweave. On Aida, you'll need more strands for even coverage.

Working from the right, bring the needle up from the back of the cloth, then down one block to the right and above. Bring it up again one block down and to the left; take it down one block above and to the right. When you want to work the next row, bring the needle up two threads right of your final stitch, and down two threads left and below. Continue working toward the right.

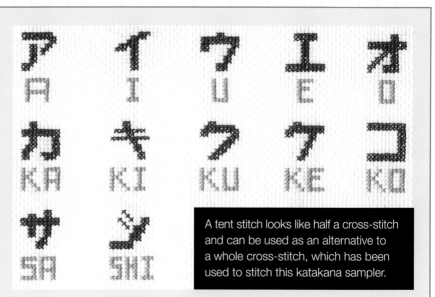

A tent stitch looks like half a cross-stitch and can be used as an alternative to a whole cross-stitch, which has been used to stitch this katakana sampler.

LAID ORIENTAL STITCH

This gives a lovely fluid texture, ideal for water or landscape. Start by making a long straight stitch, or laid thread, up to 24 threads/12 blocks long.

Bring the needle up one block right and immediately below the laid thread. Take the needle down three blocks to the left and above the laid thread. Bring it up again one block left and immediately below.

Work along the laid thread until you bring the needle down at the left end, then bring it up half a block below and lay another thread, taking the needle down immediately below the first right. Work back to the left.

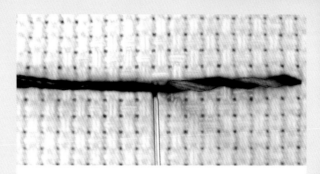

Overlapping stitches secure the long thread.

DOUBLE CROSS-STITCH

This is a useful stitch for adding texture and pattern. Make a single cross-stitch—I've worked the example over three blocks of Aida to make the method clearer, but it can be any size that suits your design—then bring the needle up in the middle of the block at the top of the cross-stitch and down directly opposite at the bottom, making an upright cross on top. You can also lengthen the straight stitches to emphasize the "star" effect, and use contrasting colors.

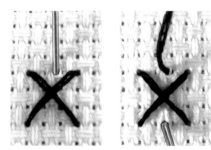

Make a basic cross.

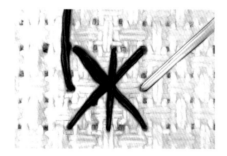

Completing the upright cross-stitch.

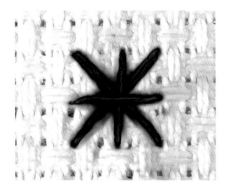

The completed stitch.

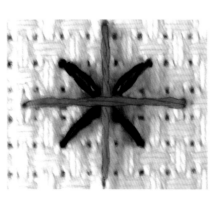

A larger upright cross makes a star.

COMPLEX STITCHES
> CREATING TONE

YOU CAN CREATE tone by varying the shade of one color across an area of cross-stitch or tent stitch, or with a suitable pattern. Here are some stitches to try out for more complex tonal effects. They can be worked on any fabric, but you may have to stitch through Aida blocks to get the right effect.

RHODES STITCH AND HALF RHODES STITCH

These chunky stitches work for basketweaves, roofs, rough grass, and ornamental fastenings. They can be worked at any scale, as long as they cover a square from 3 to 24 horizontal and vertical threads/blocks.

Decide on the size of your stitch. (I'm working over six Aida blocks.) Bring the needle up at the top right-hand corner, then down six blocks to the left, diagonally opposite. Now bring it up one block to the left of your starting point. Bring it down again one block to the right of the end of your first stitch. Continue round the square until you've covered six blocks at the top and bottom.

Starting the stitch.

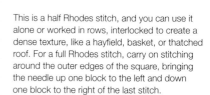

Completed half Rhodes stitch.

This is a half Rhodes stitch, and you can use it alone or worked in rows, interlocked to create a dense texture, like a hayfield, basket, or thatched roof. For a full Rhodes stitch, carry on stitching around the outer edges of the square, bringing the needle up one block to the left and down one block to the right of the last stitch.

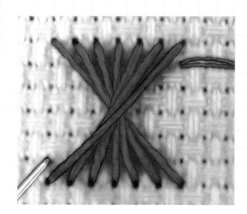

Continue working across the previous stitches.

The "star" pattern begins to form a square.

Completed Rhodes stitch.

CHAIN STITCH

You can work this stitch in close rows, curves, or single lines, and use it to suggest braids or grain.

Bring the needle up from the back of the cloth, hold the thread down in a loop with your thumb, and bring the needle down again into the same hole. Bring it up again one block below, keeping the loop under the needle, and back down into the same hole. The first loop will be secured by this stitch as long as you keep the second loop in place. Bring the needle up again one block below, keep the loop under the needle, and take it back down again. Each new stitch secures the loop of the one before. When you make your last loop, take the thread over the loop and back into the cloth, securing it with a single stitch in the center.

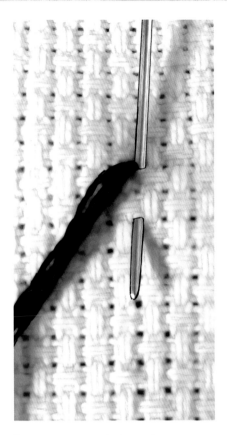

The needle secures the first loop until you make the second stitch.

PRACTICE CHART

Practice your stitches with this basic picture of a traveler in tones of blue. On soft blue or gray fabric, use laid Oriental stitch for the mountains. The river is in brick stitch, the traveler's straw hat in half Rhodes stitch and half cross-stitch, and his muffler in Rhodes stitch. Chain stitch or beads could be used for the fastening of his coat. The snowflakes, shown in electric blue to make them stand out, can be worked in white or silver.

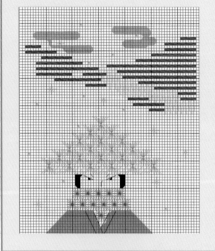

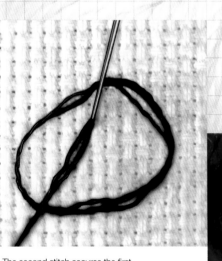

The second stitch secures the first.

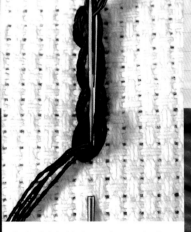

Each stitch holds the previous one in place.

Continue the steps until you've finished your chain.

ENHANCING THE IMAGE
> FABRICS AND MOUNTS

MANGA AND ANIME images are designed so that borders, margins, and backgrounds all enhance the main picture or story. Treat the mount or frame that displays your work as part of the overall design, and it will have even more impact.

First wash your finished work using mild liquid soap and cool water. Rinse well, blot with a soft towel, and then let it dry naturally. Press it, stitched side down, on a clean towel to avoid crushing your stitches.

Professional framers do good work, but you can also do it yourself—there are some excellent books and websites to guide you.

Japanese textiles are often shown unframed, mounted on fabric, and hung on rods. Even a small piece can make a sumptuous wall hanging with the right background fabric or border. A long, narrow piece can be stored as a scroll, rolled up, with rods at either end for handling.

If you plan to mount or frame your work, first fix it to a backing board. One way to do this is to fold the borders over the edges of the board and lace them together so the work is held taut and kept in place. (You can also buy self-adhesive backing boards that won't mark the fabric.)

You can then lay another mounting board on top, with openings cut as required. If you use glass or acrylic in your frame, this second board will prevent it pressing against your stitches.

Be adventurous. You can print any design directly onto fabric as a background or border for your work, using computer printable fabric available from craft suppliers. Cover boards with contrasting fabric. Add stickers or trimmings. Imagine a retro robot image in black line embroidery, with fine steel or silver gear wheels from an old watch stuck to a black mount. What about a pretty girl surrounded by ribbons and lace on a soft floral fabric mount, or a cyber creature framed with metallic paper?

Fabric with a simple design used to border your work is a great way to frame your piece.

 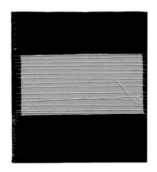

To mount your fabric, fold the borders over the edges of the board and lace them together.

Incorporating a frame into your overall design
can give your piece more impact.

BASIC DESIGN
> CHOOSING COLORS

CHOOSING THE RIGHT fabric and color is key to the success of any stitching project, but especially a manga or anime-style image. Japanese art uses a wonderful range of colors, but manga are predominantly black or monotone.

Manga anthologies are printed on cheap, rough, recycled paper, and the ink from previous use hasn't always been completely removed. The paper is dyed to mask it. You'll find pink, blue, green, and lilac pages in manga.

Ink usually tones with paper. On an off-white background, ink is black. On pink it's dull red; on blue, deep blue. If you want to use stitching to simulate the effect of screentone, you can use the same color. If you use shading, you'll need one or two darker tones of the same color, but nothing lighter than the background "paper" that will provide your highlights.

Collected stories, or *tankōbon*, are printed on better quality paper in black ink, with color splash pages. Some use textured paper.

Anime posters and magazines feature quality paper and dazzling color. High-profile projects are embellished with metallics, cutouts, or embossing. They can have lace-cut gatefolds revealing color or metallic inserts, or translucent overlays.

Aida or a coarser evenweave gives a "manga anthology" look. Smooth, white fabrics suggest a more expensive book. For a special piece you might add metallic threads, or use waste canvas to stitch on patterned or shiny fabric. For an anime project, use no more than three distinct tones of each color—a mid tone for the main area, a dark tone for shadows, and a bright one for highlights.

The black outline is vital in manga and anime art, and the style of outline changes the impact of the work. Whole stitch outlines are powerful, backstitch is more delicate, and fractionals are midway between the two. Many of the charts in this book use whole stitches only, to make them faster and easier to stitch, but even with no backstitch, outlines must be clearly defined.

The project index lists the fabric and threads used for each project. Don't feel bound by the colors and fabrics used in the examples, but if you change the size or design you'll need different quantities. Most cross-stitch charting programs will work out quantities for you.

Manga are usually printed in black and white, or monotone. The black outline is crucial to the style of manga and anime artwork.

You don't have to stick to the colors used in these projects; you can experiment with your own choices using a cross-stitch charting program. Use no more than three distinct tones for each color, though, to get the anime look.

DESIGN YOUR OWN STITCHED MANGA PAGES

DESIGNING THE LAYOUT
> CHOOSING KEY IMAGES

TO DESIGN AN effective layout, you need a clear idea of what you want to achieve. Who (or what event) is the stitching for? Is it going to be a picture, a border, a slogan? How will it be displayed? Also think about the time needed to complete it and get it framed or mounted.

With all this in mind, choose a suitable key image. Key images are the most prominent parts of your design. In a large design, you might have several key images, but for most projects one is enough.

Your key image may need editing to the right size and shape for your project. You might use only part of it. It won't necessarily be the most detailed part of the design—you could use something as simple as a silhouette for your key image.

In this page, the key image is the robot's head. The same robot is shown complete, but much smaller, in a fighting pose at the top. The close-up view and dark background convey the nobility of the robot, while the small pose emphasizes its power. The horned head may look demonic from a distance, but the face shows us a robot hero.

This chart is approximately 146 stitches wide by 177 stitches tall. At 14 HPI it will measure about 10.4 × 12.6 inches (264 × 320 mm).

Piece stitched by Chennell Hinton

This design uses a monster as the key image in a birthday greeting. It stands in front of two panels, one revealing part of its body, and a small one overlaid at the top corner that just shows its eye. Focusing attention on its strange, spiky shape and huge eyes, this plays up the monster's scary aspects, but its expression and the message it's delivering make it friendly.

This chart is approximately 106 stitches wide by 140 stitches tall. At 14 HPI it will measure about 7.6 × 10 inches (193 × 254 mm).

Piece stitched by Jenny Digney

Color can make a layout clearer—just two shades of green help make sense of the monster's complicated shape. The black and white chart without them shows the difference.

DESIGNING THE LAYOUT
> SIZE AND SHAPE

THE QUESTIONS YOU asked yourself about your layout will affect the size and shape of your design. At this stage, you should also take cost into account. Each of the projects on the CD has a key with the chart, which lists how many thread colors you'll need, and most chart design software automatically works out how much thread to use. The size of the chart dictates how much fabric you need to buy, so you can work out what your project will cost.

Once you've chosen the elements to include in your design, and decided on the overall size and shape, move them around until you find an arrangement you like. You can use graph paper to copy the finished design, scan it into the computer, and overlay a grid, or open a blank chart and add the elements you want.

Panel shapes don't have to be rectangles—try circles, segments, fan shapes, or stars. You don't need panels or background drawings; objects can "float" on a plain background, and one or two figures can make an interesting image. Here are a few ideas.

Set a single figure in a blank space with a simple border or lettering. This monster is the same one we saw on the last spread but worked in more detail, in full-color, with fractional stitches and backstitch. The broken bamboo border highlights his name in English and Japanese. The style is more refined than the whole stitch version, and the backstitch detail emphasizes the features, such as his eyes, fangs, and skin.

RYUGOGON

This chart is approximately 130 stitches wide by 147 stitches tall. At 14 HPI it will measure about 9.3 × 10.5 inches (236 × 267 mm).

Piece stitched by Emma Scorer

Set a star or heart around your key image, with supporting elements around the outside.

This chart is approximately 186 stitches wide by 181 stitches tall, about 13.3 × 12.9 inches (338 × 328 mm) at 14 HPI.

Divide the design in half, diagonally, creating a "split screen" effect.

This chart is approximately 194 stitches wide by 185 stitches tall, about 13.9 × 13.2 inches (353 × 335 mm) at 14 HPI.

You can use backstitch, full stitches, or fractional stitches to outline shapes and panels, depending on how prominent you want them to be.

Make different-sized circles or ovals, the biggest around your key image.

This chart is approximately 181 stitches wide by 183 stitches tall, about 12.9 × 13 inches (328 × 330 mm) at 14 HPI.

DESIGNING THE LAYOUT
> ROMANTIC STYLES

ROMANTIC ANIME AND manga can be sweet and bright, or moody and dramatic, so there's plenty of scope for interesting layouts. Generally speaking, the pace of the story is slower than in an action manga, and the layouts have more space, with fewer prominent sound effects and speedlines, and more decorative detail.

These elements can be used very simply, like in this monotone portrait of a girl robot. Using whole stitches, it's quick to make, but the rough heart-shaped frame, heart details, and caption make a cute package. The lettering samplers in Chapter Six give you lots of options for designing captions, or you can draft your own.

This chart is approximately 103 stitches wide by 102 stitches tall. At 14 HPI it will measure about 7.4 × 7.3 inches (188 × 185 mm).

Piece stitched by Kate Maud

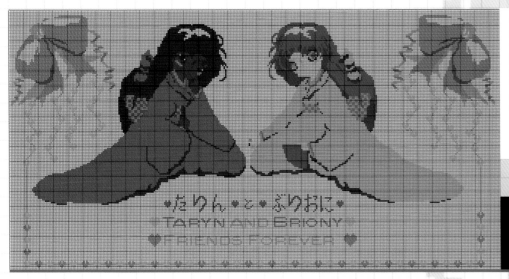

This friendship sampler is based on the Angel Princess chart in Chapter Three. The character was flipped left to right to make two girls, the position of the hands was altered on the original figure, the colors were changed, and ornate decoration was added.

This chart is approximately 336 stitches wide by 175 stitches tall. At 14 HPI it will measure about 24 × 12.5 inches (610 × 318 mm).

There's no need to stick to pastel colors—strong tones can work well in a romantic image.

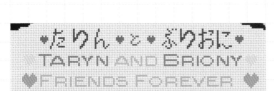

You can use decorative elements like these in other romantic images, and convert them to black and white, with the addition of some backstitch to define the ribbons and bows. Lettering in English and Japanese completes the picture. You'll find Japanese script samplers, with English translations, in Chapter Six.

For another cute, romantic arrangement, turn to Chapter Three and look at the Animal Crackers chart on page 62. Although this is a birth sampler, the swirl of friendly little stars would work as a frame for any romantic image. The Cute Accessories chart in the same chapter (page 68) will give you more ideas for romantic elements to use.

DESIGNING THE LAYOUT
> ROMANTIC STYLES

Here are two versions of a page layout, the opening of a romantic drama with simple panels and strong shading. The falling rain, stitched in white, is shown in electric blue on the chart to make it easier to see.

This chart is approximately 154 stitches wide by 182 stitches tall, about 11 × 13 inches (280 × 330 mm) at 14 HPI.

Piece stitched by Malin Stegmann McCallion

Now look at this second layout. The same images have been rearranged with an extra panel, slowing the narrative. The new panel shows that the rain hasn't started when our hero arrives. The changed heading and caption give the story a different angle—it's now boy-meets-boy. Tales of gorgeous young men falling in love are very popular with Japanese women, and there are many manga on the subject.

This chart is approximately 182 stitches wide by 196 stitches tall. At 14 HPI it will measure about 13 × 14 inches (330 × 356 mm).

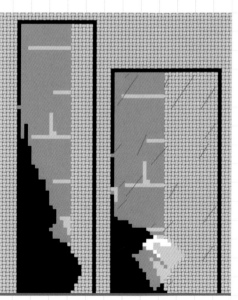

You can forget panels, titles, and decoration altogether and still make a romantic picture. This tranquil image uses the same figure as the Ronin chart in Chapter Four. A straw hat was added, and the sword hilt changed to a staff. The traveler's clothes are wrapped closely around him, and soft blue tones have replaced black. The rakish, masterless warrior becomes a pilgrim on a wintry road.

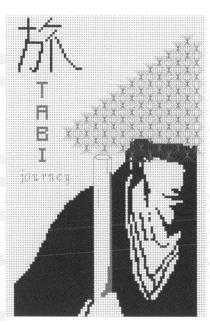

Using half Rhodes stitch for the hat gives an interesting texture, although because of the way this stitch is worked it also strays beyond the image area. This is easily hidden under a mount or frame.

The Japanese character and word for journey are set on a plain background. This would be ideal for someone setting out on a new adventure —a sabbatical, a new job, or any other life change.

This chart is approximately 82 stitches wide by 130 stitches tall. At 14 HPI it will measure about 5.9 × 9.3 inches (150 × 236 mm).

DESIGNING THE LAYOUT
> ACTION STYLES

THIS IMAGE OF a robot could be used facing either way. This direction is best for an English-language comic layout, where the images and story flow left to right. Japanese is read from right to left, so Japanese comics arrange their images to lead the reader through the story from the right.

We've seen how background elements and lettering can enhance a key image. This chart uses the same elements but adds a formal title frame, plus a signature graphic of the robot's head in a simplified style. Shown here stitched on blue Aida, it's in whole stitches and one color, making it quick to stitch.

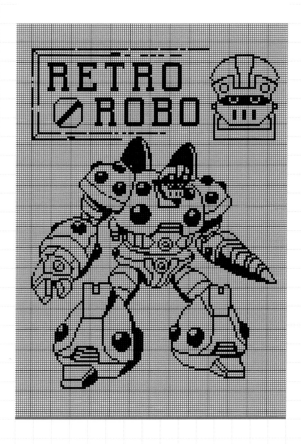

This chart is approximately 126 stitches wide by 166 stitches tall. At 14 HPI it will measure about 9 × 11.9 inches (229 × 302 mm).

Piece stitched by Michelle Hurst

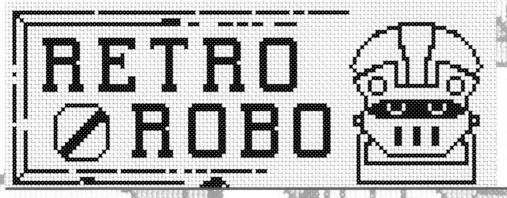

The title uses a formal alphabet to enhance the retro look. It's the kind of lettering you might see on old trains or buses, and the frame echoes the strip framing on the panels of old vehicles. It's broken in places to give a slightly worn, aged effect.

The heading is completed with an outline graphic of the robot's head facing front. This turns the title into a logo, reinforcing the robot's image like a brand label. The original design has him looking sideways, so to make the front-facing version I used the proportions of the original as a guide and counted stitches to get the various parts the right size in relation to each other. To keep the head symmetrical, I charted one side, then flipped and pasted it using the Edit menu.

One of the big missiles mounted on the robot's back breaks the frame. Breaking up lines and panels makes a page livelier and less rigid. The lettering is regularly spaced to keep up a sense of formality, but the bottom line starts farther in, so as not to make it too static. The space is filled with a very simple shape that recalls old-fashioned nuts and bolts.

DESIGNING THE LAYOUT
> ACTION STYLES

You can still make a calm, reflective image using action-style elements. Even giant robots have their quiet moments.

Here's an image that portrays two very different robots as buddies.

The background could be fully stitched or worked on blue cloth. The starry sky gives more than one possible story—are they taking a late-night stroll, heading home after a heroic exploit, or soaring through the air about to start one? It's good to leave something to the onlooker's imagination.

This is a more detailed image of the retro-style robot from the previous page. The medium-sized version of the boy robot is a less detailed chart but fits well here.

This chart is approximately 175 stitches wide by 238 stitches tall. On 14 HPI it will measure about 12.5 × 17 inches (318 × 432 mm).

Piece stitched by Nikki Thompson

I charted more of the big robot at this scale, because I wasn't sure exactly what story I wanted the image to tell. To begin with, I thought about putting the little robot lower down and closer to the center of the picture, heading upward to deliver a punch to that huge jaw. With the addition of a few speedlines and a sound effect, the story would have been very different to that of the pair on the opposite page.

For those who love huge, full-color anime posters, you could simply drop the Streets chart into the upper background of this image and flood-fill the vacant spaces with a neutral or bluish gray to represent the roadway. A massive project like this would keep even an experienced stitcher busy, but since it uses only whole stitches, it's not too difficult. There's nothing wrong with delicate, feminine needlework, but this piece demonstrates it isn't the only option.

This chart is approximately 285 stitches wide by 423 stitches tall.
On 14 HPI it will measure about 20.4 × 30.2 inches (518 × 767 mm).

This chart is approximately 285 stitches wide by 423 stitches tall.
On 14 HPI it will measure about 20.4 × 30.2 inches (518 × 767 mm).

REFINING THE ROUGH LAYOUT
> COMPOSITION

A MORE COMPLEX layout needs especially careful planning to make sure the key images aren't lost in a mass of detail. Take time to experiment for the best results. Here, the same design components have been worked into two different page layouts, demonstrating the importance of balance within the composition.

This first draft of a big double-page manga spread is laid out Japanese style, from right to left.

I made a background of ruined buildings and roughly cut it to fit one page. The Retro Robo from page 44 was pasted in place. The ruins were pasted on top, and reworked until the robot could be seen behind them without obscuring the outline.

For the second page I used another section of street, two small Super Robos, and a huge fist modified from the large Super Robo chart (page 36), with sound effects and speedlines added. Everything was recolored in blue, and a text box suggests the beginning of a story.

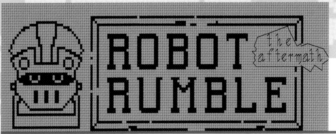

The title and logo above the robot were modified from the Retro Robo logo on pages 44–45.

The outline and lettering styles are varied but work well together. Now the design needs tidying up.

On the revised version, the spread is better balanced, with the robot images and text forming two diagonals that lead the eye from one page to the next.

This chart is approximately 350 stitches wide by 203 stitches tall, about 25 × 14.5 inches (635 × 368 mm) at 14 HPI.

ROBOTS RULE!

The small text box is centered at the top of the spread, and the images and text have been centered on their own pages so they work independently. A line of free-floating text on the left page completes the story. The title should normally be the largest text on any image, so the lettering was adapted by shortening the top half of the characters by one row and the lower half by two rows.

REFINING THE ROUGH LAYOUT
> SOUND EFFECTS

THE JAPANESE WORD for sound effects is *gitaigo*, meaning onomatopoeia—words that sound like the things they describe. Manga artists can make them not just sound but look like the things they describe, and they are as carefully designed and placed as any characters.

You can put sound effects anywhere and in any direction as long as it fits your design. They can be written in Japanese or in English, but the style, size, and placing should echo what you want them to do.

A loud, powerful sound like *BAN*—Japanese for an enormous bang or explosion—should be written in big, solid characters. This robot's foot, descending to earth with a thump, has the effect written in large, Japanese characters, with debris flying and impact lines. The foot breaks the panel frame and even makes the sound effect jump—look at the jagged shapes and the tiny pieces flying off the lettering.

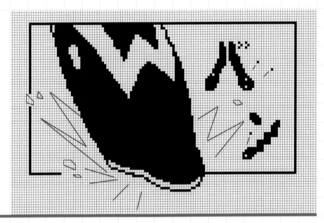

This chart is approximately 115 stitches wide by 62 stitches tall. At 14 HPI it will measure about 8.2 × 4.4 inches (208 × 112 mm).

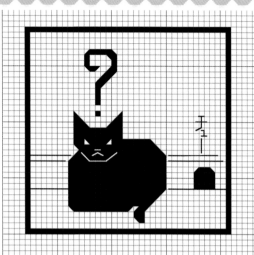

A very small sound, like the squeak of a mouse—*chuu* in Japanese—would be written in very small letters, and the mouse might not even be visible. The sound effect could stand in for the animal, with the sound written in a corner or under a chair, and a cat looking puzzled nearby. (Japanese cats say *nyan* for meow.) Where a sound effect's origin is missing or not obvious, a small line can be placed nearby to indicate the direction it's coming from.

This chart is approximately 39 stitches wide by 38 stitches tall. At 14 HPI it will measure about 2.8 × 2.7 inches (71 × 69 mm).

Repetitive sounds are usually written several times across the panel, or even several panels. Gunshots or explosions (*don*), or loud knocking (*dan*), might be spaced apart to indicate several single sounds, or run together. Where gunshots are written dramatically, sounds like wind in trees are usually shown in a softer style.

Drawn-out sounds, like "Aaaah," are shown by a line trailing from the end of the effect, by leaving long spaces between characters, or by elongating the characters themselves. Most sound effects are written in katakana, but some appear in hiragana. Most important of these is *shiin*, meaning absolute silence. Look at Chapter Six for examples of sound effects and for katakana and hiragana characters.

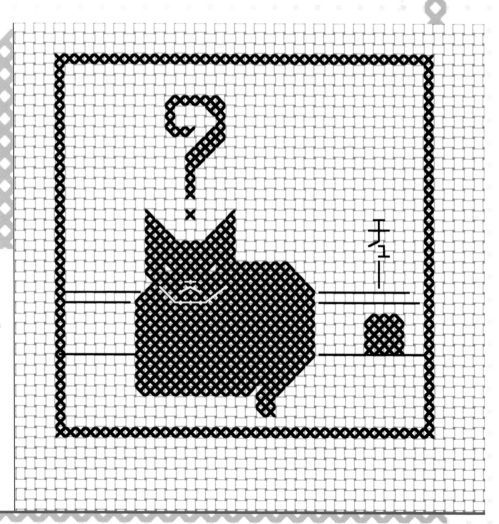

REFINING THE ROUGH LAYOUT
> DIALOGUE AND LETTERING

ADDING SCRIPT TO your image isn't essential, but it will personalize it. Greetings and messages can be integrated into the picture and put into a speech balloon, as in the monster birthday greeting on page 37, or framed, like in the Retro Robo and Robot Rumble designs (pages 44 and 49).

Make sure that text doesn't overwhelm the image. Manga and anime are visual storytelling—even when there's a message to get across, the text shouldn't dominate.

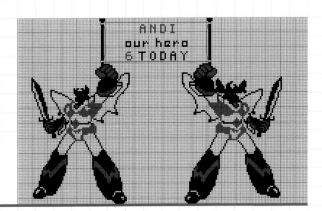

Japanese artists use lettering as part of the image.

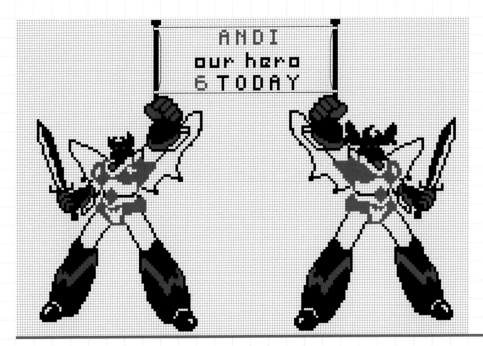

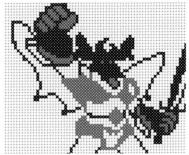

A huge robot could have someone's nickname or initials stencilled on his arm or chest, a hoarding could show a message, or two characters could carry a banner with a greeting.

This chart is approximately 190 stitches wide by 140 stitches long, about 14 × 10 inches (356 × 254 mm) at 14 HPI.

Lettering can be used as a decorative element in its own right. It forms the background to this three-color image of a pair of twins: a samurai—you can tell by his hairstyle and the *mon*, or crest, on his neatly wrapped kimono—and a ronin or masterless sword-for-hire. The same logo forms both title and background, where the text is repeated and flipped for the background, and highlighted in red for the page title.

Lettering is often used like this for covers or splash pages. For a romantic or nostalgic image it could be worked in half cross-stitch or using only one thread, to make it more ethereal. For a horror or punk image, try glow-in-the-dark or fluorescent thread.

The type of line you choose for your lettering is as important in defining the style of your image as the lines you choose to define panels or figures. You can use whole stitches, fractionals, or backstitch, in one, two, or more threads. Varying the line lets you give text different levels of impact.

This chart is approximately 98 stitches wide by 161 stitches long, about 7 × 11.5 inches (178 × 292 mm) at 14 HPI.

Piece stitched by Donna Harris

CUTE CREATURES AND CHARACTERS

EXPLAINING CUTE MANGA
> KAWAII TIPS AND GUIDELINES

Kawaii is known worldwide as Japanese for cute. Characters like Osamu Tezuka's heroic robot Astro Boy, and brands like Hello Kitty, Japan's unofficial ambassador of girlie culture, have helped to create an international appreciation of the enchanting, wide-eyed icons of innocence that are so important in manga and anime.

Japan has a yearly festival where children aged three, five, and seven are dressed in formal kimono and presented at shrines. Small children are always cute, so perhaps this enchanting annual parade of tots in tiny versions of grown-up costume has created a fondness for cute imagery in general. You'll often hear the word "-*chan*," Japanese for dear or darling, added after the names of cute creatures and small children.

Animals are used in cute creations, either as the main characters or in supporting roles to children, angels, or magical beings. Sometimes they have special powers, like the ability to speak or fly. Magic is often part of cute imagery. *Little Witch Sally* was one of the most popular animated TV shows in Japan in the 1960s; the adventures of a little witch sent to live among humans enchanted Japanese schoolgirls and started a trend that continues today. Anime and manga about cute fairies, magicians, and angels venturing into our world are common.

Color is key to making an image kawaii. Pure, clear colors create a playful mood. Paler tones add a wistful element, brighter ones an upbeat atmosphere. Yet, as we've seen with the Rogirl portrait on page 40, it's possible to create kawaii images in black and white, or monotone, with the right design and accessories. Animals, toys and games, flowers, hearts, stars, ribbons, and lace make excellent backdrops for cute characters.

Shapes should be rounded and soft, outlines suited to the character. Fine lines create an ethereal impression, while stronger lines have more impact. You can make cute characters using whole stitch, but fractional stitches make softer shapes. There are charts and projects in this chapter using just whole stitch, or fractionals and backstitch, so you can make your own kind of cute stitching.

EXPLAINING CUTE MANGA
> CHIBI AND "SD" FIGURES

CHIBI AND "SD," or "super deformed," characters are archetypes of kawaii culture. Chibi is Japanese for small, and these characters are childlike, with rounded bodies, short arms and legs, and oversized heads.

All kinds of characters can be made chibi, including adult action heroes and heroines. Super deformed characters are more manic and muscular than chibis, and can have slightly longer limbs. They're used for action scenes, poses that don't work for short limbs, or comedy.

Don't get too bogged down in the detail, especially when making a small image. The important thing is to get the proportions right. Once you have the basic, simple body shape you can vary it by changing hair, clothes, and limbs. A little backstitch can redefine hands or faces.

Each character is approximately 53 stitches wide by 56 stitches tall, around 3.8 × 4 inches (97 × 102 mm) at 14 HPI. The schoolgirls are 83 stitches wide by 89 tall, about 5.9 × 6.4 inches (150 × 163 mm) at 14 HPI.

Piece stitched by Laura Riley and Caroline McFadden

This collection of chibi cuties, each less than four inches tall, was charted from two designs using the Copy and Flip Left to Right commands on the Edit menu, and giving the characters different costumes and hairstyles.

Use them in cards, pictures, and manga pages, or as inspiration for your own characters—try changing their expressions using the effects charts in Chapter Five. I changed the legs and hairstyles to design these boisterous classmates. Here, the girls are stitched on pale gray, 28-count Jobelan.

This ferocious little *oni*, a Japanese demon, is big enough to allow for plenty of detail, but keeping it bold avoids making the overall picture too fussy. Fractional stitches help to pick up the details in his frowning face, muscular torso, and elaborate costume. Varied outlines and bold shading make a dynamic picture.

This chart is approximately 119 stitches wide by 158 stitches tall, about 8.5 × 11.3 inches (216 × 287 mm) at 14 HPI.

CUTE CHARACTERS
> ANGEL PRINCESS

MANGA SPLASH PAGES use full color, but because of the technical requirements of anime, colors are restricted to three tones: a light tone, a midtone, and a dark tone for shadows. Black outlines are also used. This style developed because it made animation simpler and cheaper; it also simplifies color choices for needlework.

This cute little character is typical of the color splash-page images in girls' comics. The shading on her kimono is blocky and simple. The focus is on her eyes, stitched in three tones of green with white highlights, and two tones of gray for the lashes and shadows; and on her hair, in three tones of corn gold. To stitch the whole figure, working a couple of hours most evenings, would take about three weeks, so I selected the head and shoulders to make a portrait for a quicker result.

The softness of the picture is enhanced by keeping backstitch to a minimum and using softer colors, so the shapes are gentler and less definite. The closed fan in her left hand is defined in gold, and her right hand and the collar of her pale pink inner kimono are outlined in backstitch for definition.

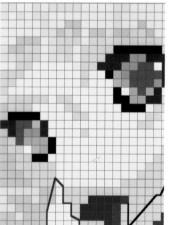

The pink backstitch for her lips was given extra definition by going over it twice—so there are four threads instead of two, giving a slightly plumper look to the mouth. The stitch is straight, but I've kept the tension quite relaxed and then used a tiny stitch in the center to pull it down just a little, giving it a very gentle curve. Be prepared to experiment with this until you get the expression you want—you might like to practice on some scrap cloth before stitching onto the finished face.

The larger chart is approximately 148 stitches wide by 108 stitches tall, about 10.6 × 7.7 inches (269 × 196 mm) on 14 HPI. The portrait is 61 stitches wide by 57 stitches tall, about 4.4 × 4.1 inches (112 × 104 mm) at 14 HPI.

Piece stitched by Helen McCarthy

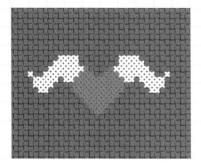

I've added a tiny winged heart to this piece, which I've used as a motif for the background, so the princess has hearts fluttering around her head. Any romantic frame or decoration—such as stitched ribbons or flowers—would work equally well with this picture.

With a few changes, my design became a sampler celebrating an 18th birthday. It was stitched using DMC Satin thread S211 mixed with stranded cotton to give the kimono a rich sheen.

STEFFI·CHAN

our darling daughter
STEPHANIE
♥   ♥

ABCDEFGHIJKLMNOPQRSTUVWXYZ
abcdefghijklmnopqrstuvwxyz

The background is a gorgeous sky blue and white Aida that suggests cloudy spring skies, with a pearlized thread woven through for a hint of sparkle. Most pearlized thread is plastic and needs extra care when pressing the finished work to make sure the iron doesn't melt it.

The chart is approximately 261 stitches wide by 162 tall, about 18.6 × 11.6 inches (472 × 295 mm) at 14 HPI.

Piece stitched by Sarah Broadhurst

CUTE CHARACTERS
> ANIMAL CRACKERS

THE ARRIVAL OF a new baby is an important event, and this big, bold group of cheerful creatures makes a wonderful birth sampler. I charted these cute animal friends using whole stitch, fractionals, and backstitch to define each figure in a slightly different way.

To make the four separate charts into one design, I pasted them into a new blank chart. I knew the big, cuddly bear would be the key image, so I set the lettering immediately below him. Using the Cut, Paste, and Undo commands, I tried various combinations until I was happy with the design.

This chart is approximately 214 stitches wide by 295 stitches tall, about 15.3 × 21.1 inches (387 × 536 mm) at 14 HPI.

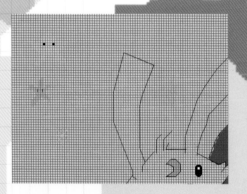

Fractional stitches emphasize the roughness of fur, while backstitch brings out the expression on each animal's face and the detail of their markings. Different kinds of line also help to suggest different personalities for the creatures. The dog is stitched with a combination of whole stitches and fractionals, to suggest an energetic, friendly character. Strong outlines make him stand out, while the shy rabbit is outlined in delicate backstitch. To see what a difference the outline style makes, compare the dog and bunny stitched in whole crosses on pages 64–65, or the cat's head on page 20, stitched with a fractional outline along the lower face, whereas here all the detail is in backstitch.

The scattering of friendly little stars helps to pull the design together and links the flying cat to his earthbound friends.

The arrangement leaves plenty of space for a baby's name and birthdate. I love to include hearts on birth samplers, but you could use blocks or diamonds instead. To stitch a longer message—perhaps two sets of names for twins—you could choose a smaller alphabet from one of the samplers in Chapter Six, or move the date up and run your lettering right across the bottom of the image, allowing the dog's paw to overlap it.

MIX AND MATCH
> CUTE CHARACTERS

I love these animals just as they are, but I couldn't resist making a scary version of the bear, with a grumpy little cat skeleton in his stomach. Here, Skelecat and Bear's teeth and eyes are all stitched in DMC's glow-in-the-dark thread—perfect for a bit of spooky fun in a child's bedroom! Bad Bear was stitched in red on black Aida.

This chart is approximately 124 stitches wide by 128 stitches tall, about 8.9 × 9.1 inches (226 × 231 mm) at 14 HPI.

Piece stitched by Marcia Kiley

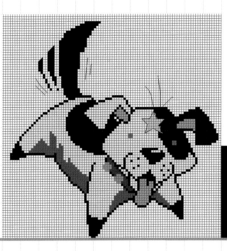

This friendly dog is stitched in whole stitch on white Aida, with a little backstitch for the speedlines around his wagging tail and to define the star on his forehead. It was difficult to chart the star accurately in fractionals; the backstitch helps to even the outline and give it more impact.

This chart is approximately 90 stitches wide by 91 stitches tall, about 6.4 × 6.5 inches (163 × 165 mm) at 14 HPI.

Piece stitched by Nikki Thompson

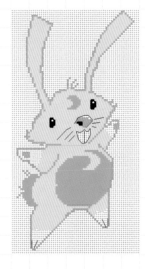

This little bunny is stitched on white Aida, mixing DMC's pearlized Light Effects thread E818 with pink stranded cotton so his fur gleams. Special threads aren't always as supple as cotton, and it takes extra effort to get the stitches looking neat, but they give interesting effects. The pastel outline softens the image; it looks crisper outlined in backstitch, and stronger worked in whole stitch with a black outline.

These charts are approximately 65 stitches wide by 134 stitches tall, about 4.6 × 9.6 inches (117 × 244 mm) at 14 HPI.

Piece stitched by Helen Vale

The flying cat on page 63 is detailed with backstitch, helping to define his features. His portrait is featured in Chapter One in different colors, and there's also a black and white version on page 67.

This chart is approximately 101 stitches wide by 111 stitches tall. At 14 HPI it will measure about 7.2 × 7.9 inches (183 × 201 mm).

MIX AND MATCH
> CUTE CHARACTERS

RYUGOGON THE MONSTER first appeared in Chapter Two, but he and egg-shaped monster Chupi make a charming pair in these two full-color pictures. You can always change the colors to personalize your characters, but remember to use no more than three distinct tones per color to get the anime look.

Chupi is worked on Zweigart white evenweave, Ryugogon on Charles Craft salt-colored Carolina linen. Pure linen is more expensive than even the best quality evenweave, but cotton-linen mixes like Carolina look good and are easy to work with.

This chart is approximately 130 stitches wide by 148 stitches tall, about 9.3 × 10.5 inches (236 × 267 mm) at 14 HPI.

Piece stitched by Emma Scorer

Linen and evenweaves are good choices for projects like these, with lots of fractional stitches. You can make fractional stitches on Aida, but you have to split each block of threads by pushing your needle through the center. It can be difficult to keep all the fractionals exactly the same size. If you're stitching over two threads of evenweave, there's a hole in the center of every block, making fractionals easy.

Fractional stitches give smoother outlines and more definition—look at the whole stitch chart of Chupi, right, to see the difference. For whole cross-stitches, evenweave works as well as Aida. It's a matter of personal preference, and what best fits your project and budget.

This chart is approximately 109 stitches wide by 107 stitches tall. At 14 HPI it will measure about 7.8 × 7.7 inches (198 × 196 mm).

Cute creatures usually get stitched in color, but monotone versions can be very effective. Here's a black and white version of the Skycat to get you started. It would look wonderful stitched in silver or white on dark fabric, with a scattering of stars from Chupi's chart in silver and a crescent moon from the Cute Accessories chart on page 68.

This chart is approximately 101 stitches wide by 111 stitches tall, about 7.2 × 7.9 inches (183 × 201 mm) at 14 HPI.

This chart is approximately 154 stitches wide by 161 stitches tall, about 11 × 11.5 inches (279 × 292 mm) at 14 HPI.

Piece stitched by Emma Scorer

MIX AND MATCH
> CUTE ACCESSORIES

THIS IS A collection of images for borders, backgrounds, and/or adding detail to your designs—animals, moons and stars, Japanese parasols, lanterns, fans and wooden geta sandals, and cherry blossoms. You'll see cherry blossoms in many anime and manga. It's a symbol of youth, beauty, change, and impermanence.

Umbrella top view

Umbrella closed

Fans

Dragonfly

Dragonflies

Umbrella bottom view

Cherry blossoms

SAKURA NO HANA

Teddy bear

Dragonfly side view

Geta sandals

Leaves

Dragonfly

Fish

Shells and jellyfish

Moon, stars, and birds

Butterfly side view

Bow

Bunny rabbits

Umbrella side view

Butterfly

Butterfilies side view

Bow

Mice

Gift boxes

Butterfly

Butterfly

This picture was stitched on pink evenweave. Here's how I put it together: First I copied the red umbrella from the accessories chart into a new chart, twice, editing the black lines on the twin umbrellas to make sure everything matched up. Next, I pasted two heads from the chibi chums chart on page 58. I tidied up the stitches using the Cut and Paste, and Erase modes. Then I added geta sandals from the accessories chart, erasing the top sections to fit them under the umbrellas.

I colored the faces and added a hand from page 58, drawing a new kimono sleeve with threads added from the Palette menu.

This chart is 118 stitches wide by 98 stitches tall, about 8.5 × 7 inches (216 × 178 mm) at 14 HPI.

Piece stitched by Caroline McFadden

Now we have two cute little characters in traditional costume, peeping cheekily over their huge umbrellas. You could use this for a wedding or engagement greeting, with the couple's names and the date on the umbrellas, or as a birth sampler, or friendship gift.

To expand it, I opened a new chart, copied and pasted the dragonflies from the Accessories chart several times, then tidied up any cut or duplicated stitches. I cut and pasted the figures and added a summery blue background.

These charts are approximately 163 stitches wide by 179 stitches tall. At 14 HPI they will measure about 11.6 × 12.8 inches (295 × 325 mm).

Adding a lantern from the accessories chart and changing the background color to a darker blue creates the impression of a summer night, perhaps after a festival. I left more space around the image to suggest encroaching shadows.

MIX AND MATCH
> CUTE CYBER BEINGS

ROBOTS CAN BE menacing, but these two cybercuties are friendly and fun. Rogirl and Roboy's black and white portraits appear in Chapters Two and Five, respectively, but here they are shown in full color.

Charted smaller and in black and white, Rogirl is much simpler and less detailed, but she still makes a charming picture. The smallest Roboy was charted in color, but you could convert either one to make a pair of portraits or to stitch their own manga adventure.

This chart is approximately 92 stitches wide by 129 stitches tall, about 6.6 × 9.2 inches (168 × 234 mm) on 14 HPI.

Here, Rogirl has been stitched on pale cream Belfast linen, and although the chart uses only whole stitches, there's plenty of detail in this big image. Stitched on 14/28-count fabric from the largest charts, Rogirl and Roboy would make an impressive pair.

The Rogirl chart is approximately 124 stitches wide by 252 stitches tall. At 14 HPI it will measure about 8.9 × 18 inches (226 × 457 mm).

Piece stitched by Nadia Osman

This medium-size Roboy was stitched on white Aida. To give his metallic skin a sheen, DMC Light Effects pearlescent thread in blue (E3747) was mixed with pale gray stranded cotton. The dimensions of the finished stitching are closer to the large Rogirl chart, because his pose takes up more space.

This small Roboy chart is approximately 80 stitches wide by 120 stitches tall, about 5.7 × 8.6 inches (145 × 218 mm) at 14 HPI.

This medium Roboy chart is approximately 127 stitches wide by 228 stitches tall, about 9.1 × 16.3 inches (231 × 414 mm) at 14 HPI.

Piece stitched by Karen Hall

This large Roboy chart is 173 stitches wide by 311 stitches tall, about 12.4 × 22.2 inches (315 × 564 mm) at 14 HPI.

CUTE MANGA PAGES
> USING THE CHARTS

IN THE LAST two chapters we've made striking pages from single characters, and combined individual charts with background elements and accessories. Making your own pictures and projects is fun, whether you use the computer to speed up the task of copying images and arranging them onto a new chart, or do it the traditional way with colored pencils and graph paper.

When copying and pasting from chart to chart on the computer, you may find you pick up parts of adjacent images that you don't need for your work. It's easy to erase these using the Erase function or the Edit menu. You may also find that you get some unexpected distortions when you copy and paste, or flip left to right or upside down. I check the whole design every time I make a change, then tidy up anything that needs amending. Make sure everything is as you want it, and then save before you go on to the next stage. If something goes disastrously wrong, the Undo function will let you undo your last actions.

Here's a little chart celebrating the last day of school, chibi style. It uses two different styles of lettering in headings, a more formal one for the title and the small Dash alphabet for the main caption. The smaller captions and dialogue are in backstitch.

I adapted the school uniform figures from page 58, changing hairstyles, altering legs to make them appear to be running forward, and adding backstitch to suggest school doors and steps. I changed the stitches in the boy's hand to let him hold a briefcase.

This chart is approximately 136 stitches wide by 91 stitches tall, about 9.7 × 6.5 inches (246 × 165 mm) at 14 HPI.

The panel that introduces the story was very easy to draw. Again, the classroom background is represented with just a few backstitches to suggest a desk, a book, and a clock. Make this classic black and white manga by removing the colors one by one, replacing some with black to make a strong image.

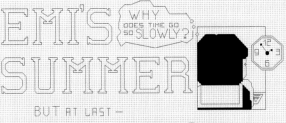

These charts are approximately 161 stitches wide by 197 stitches tall, about 11.5 × 14.1 inches (292 × 358 mm) at 14 HPI.

ACTION AND ADVENTURE

EXPLAINING MENACING MECHA
> HOT-HEADED HEROES

Mecha is the word that anime and manga fans use for any mechanical object, but it's most often associated with giant robots. There are two main kinds of robots in manga and anime—those with artificial intelligence, which can act independently, and those that must be operated by a person.

The styles and designs of robots vary hugely, from simple, box-like tin-plate robots to towering creatures recalling suits of armor or insect carapaces. Capturing mechanical detail in stitching can be a huge challenge, and unless you're working on a very large scale, it's usually best to choose a simple overall design to avoid your work becoming too fussy. An action-packed image needs to allow room for the action to be appreciated.

The same applies to stitching heroes and villains. Unless you're working on a huge scale, like the stunning Samurai Girl on page 84, you need to simplify the picture. You'll notice that anime and manga artists often leave out unnecessary details to focus on key images and vital design elements.

The Ronin charts on pages 82–83 take this to an extreme level, breaking the image down into a stark collection of pixels, yet still conveying character and a narrative, or story.

Facial expressions have an important role to play in action images. Using only whole stitches works at a large scale, but to make smaller images, backstitch is a useful tool. Plan it carefully and work a small sample to look at the different effects you can get by using two or three strands instead of one, or by using different colors instead of outlining only in black. For mouths, using three strands and relaxing the tension slightly gives a softer shape, while using colored thread mimics lipstick.

You can change skin tones, hair colors, and details to create different effects—look at the High School Yakuza and Yoyo Trio (above) on pages 80–81. Most charting programs allow you to change cloth color onscreen, so try varying your background color. Keep colors strong and emphasize the contrast between light and dark for a powerful, eye-catching image.

EXPLAINING MENACING MANGA
> BIG EYES, BIG EXPLOSIONS

BIG EYES AND big hair didn't start with anime and manga. There are many examples in traditional Japanese art.

This design for a *hannya* mask, with staring eyes, streaming hair, and horns, is based on a character from classical Noh theater. A monster's image was thought to protect the home from evil spirits, so this would make an unusual housewarming gift, as well as adding drama to your projects. Stitch on colored fabric to save time.

This chart is approximately 194 stitches wide by 180 tall. At 14 HPI it will measure about 13.9 × 12.9 inches (354 × 328 mm).

The face of this girl assassin was charted much smaller than the Hannya chart. Her eyes and mouth rely on carefully placed stitches to depict her expression properly.

The mouth has a combination of whole stitch, fractionals, and backstitch in red and black. Follow the chart carefully for the outline, and fill with backstitch so that the whole cloth is covered. The filling stitches should radiate from the line between her upper and lower lip. The white half cross-stitch on the nose provides a vital highlight. When stitching facial expressions, don't be afraid to unpick and re-stitch, but take care not to damage surrounding stitches.

This chart is approximately 152 stitches wide by 170 stitches tall, about 10.9 × 12.1 inches (277 × 307 mm) at 14 HPI.

This cheerful image shows a chibi high school girl making a classic cheeky face, seen in hundreds of anime and manga. Big eyes and big hair emphasize the comical expression, and, using only whole stitches, it's not difficult to capture the naughty look of this design. Try working just her face alongside the hannya mask for a pair of pictures that sum up 500 years of Japanese art.

The full-length chart is approimately 74 stitches wide by 149 stitches tall, about 5.3 × 10.6 inches (135 × 269 mm) at 14 HPI. The face chart is approximately 183 stitches wide by 198 tall, about 13.1 × 14.1 inches (333 × 358 mm) at 14 HPI.

ACTION AND ADVENTURE
> HIGH SCHOOL RUMBLE

JAPANESE HIGH SCHOOL students wear distinctive uniforms. Boys' uniforms are based on old military school outfits, and girls wear either a variation on the popular sailor suit, or a skirt and blazer.

Here the feisty girl assassin from page 79 has been re-dressed in the sailor suit I used for the chibi characters on page 58, making her a high school yakuza.

To alter the costume, I followed the lines of the original outfit—the sailor's collar is crumpled to fit over the character's raised shoulder, and the skirt pleats follow the direction of the narrower split skirt on the Two-Gun Girl, but with more movement. I swapped the futuristic geta-style trainers for sensible school shoes and baggy white socks. I also simplified her white gloves and changed her hairstyle, but the big guns and their blasts are the same.

This chart is approximately 152 stitches wide by 170 stitches tall, about 10.9 x 12.1 (227 × 307 mm) at 14 HPI.

I used the same design to make this picture of three high school friends with yoyos. The yoyo is a favorite schoolgirl weapon in many Japanese dramas, but these three girls are just having fun. Notice the different skintones and hair colors, and their cheeky expressions.

Framing the girls in a wide oval makes an attractive panel and also means you don't have to stitch the lower bodies, giving a quicker result. The background was filled in with pale blue and white to suggest a sunny sky over a school playground. In order to transform this into a monotone image, why not try Chapter One's special stitches, or the stitched screentone patterns shown in the next chapter?

The eyes are outlined in backstitch, with no fractionals, and are slightly smaller than the original. The mouths are narrower. Using backstitch instead of fractionals alters the overall mood and impact of the design.

This chart is approximately 152 stitches wide by 87 stitches tall, about 10.9 × 6.2 inches (277 × 157 mm) at 14 HPI.

Piece stitched by Amanda Wood

GRAPHIC ELEMENTS
> RONIN

CLASSIC MANGA DERIVES much of its impact from its simplicity. The starkness of black ink on plain paper makes an arresting image, and focusing on essentials like the pose and expression, rather than the details of costume and background, can create a powerful impression.

Sometimes, adding in a small area of detail and one or two extra colors can sharpen the image even further. In this image of a masterless samurai—a ronin—gripping his sword, you can see how the green eye, red headband, and sword handle powerfully enhance the stark black and white figure. With only three colors on white, the stitching should be relatively quick and easy, but the impact of the finished work is quite striking and potent.

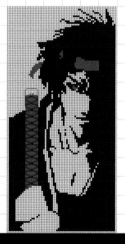

Just four colors—black, red, green, and white—create this powerful image. The chart is approximately 65 stitches wide by 135 stitches tall. At 14 HPI it will measure about 4.6 × 9.6 inches (117 × 244 mm).

Stitched by Helen McCarthy

You can have fun playing with different color combinations and adding and removing detail. To make things even simpler, eliminate one of the colors. Making the eye red also adds a demonic element to the picture—if you want to enhance it further, give your ronin horns.

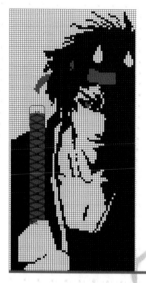 

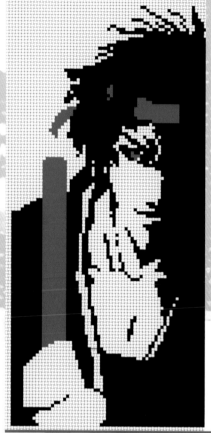 

A rough, basic graphic technique using only whole cross-stitches for the majority of the picture gives it a contemporary edge. If you really hate doing backstitch you can simply leave it out; the image will still be powerful, but you'll finish it faster.

A different background color could also be used—black and red look arresting. If you want to simplify the sword and minimize backstitch, just use it to outline the shape.

The space at the top left-hand side allows you to add in details, such as a date, greeting, or extra imagery. Here I've added a bamboo motif.

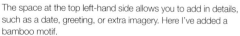

MIX AND MATCH
> SAMURAI CHARA

Working on a large scale with whole stitches is easy and adds impact. This fantasy samurai girl is very detailed and large, yet uses backstitch only to define the eyelids. The modeling of the figure is achieved through simple anime-style shading.

The full-length chart is approximately 272 stitches wide by 458 stitches tall. At 14 HPI it will measure about 19.4 × 32.7 inches (493 × 831 mm).

Here, the hannya mask from page 78 has been added to provide even more drama to this image of the fierce samurai girl.

This chart is approximately 374 stitches wide by 520 stitches tall. At 14 HPI it will measure about 26.7 × 37.1 inches (678 × 942 mm).

This monotone chart is approximately 120 stitches wide by 200 tall. At 14 HPI it will measure about 8.6 × 14.3 inches (218 × 363 mm).

MIX AND MATCH
> MONSTER CHARA

A FANTASY SAMURAI needs a suitable opponent. This monster was designed to menace the samurai girl, though of course you can use him alone or menacing anything you like.

The detail of the twin eye sockets couldn't be charted in whole stitches on the smaller chart, so there are some fractionals. If you decide to make the smaller chart black and white, define the outlines with backstitch before you take out the colors.

You can also emphasize the monster's menace by adding a bold, graphic sound effect. This effect—*gyaaa*, a long drawn-out shriek or scream—is charted in two sizes. Here I used the larger one.

The larger chart is approximately 57 by 122 stitches, about 4.1 × 8.7 inches (104 × 221 mm) at 14 HPI.

The smaller chart is approximately 36 by 82 stitches, about 2.6 × 5.9 inches (66 × 150 mm) at 14 HPI.

The combined chart is approximately 237 by 277 stitches, about 16.9 × 19.8 inches (429 × 503 mm) at 14 HPI.

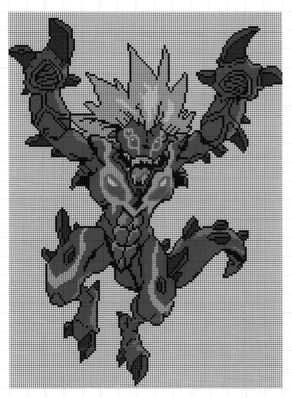

This chart is approximately 273 stitches wide by 277 stitches tall, about 19.5 × 19.8 inches (495 × 503 mm) at 14 HPI.

This chart is approximately 140 stitches wide by 177 stitches tall, about 10 × 12.6 inches (254 × 320 mm) at 14 HPI.

MIX AND MATCH
> MECHA

SUPER ROBO APPEARED as a portrait head and small figure in Chapter Two. This style of robot was very popular in the 1970s and 1980s.

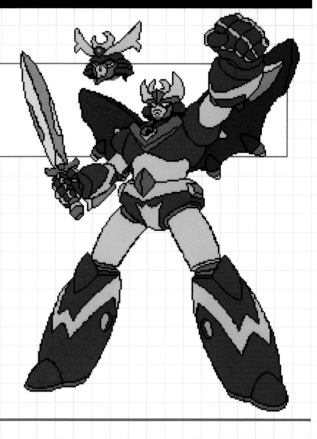

There's a little backstitch detail on these robot faces. There are two head designs so you can choose your favorite or stitch both versions if you prefer.

This chart is approximately 192 stitches wide by 249 stitches tall, about 13.7 × 17.8 inches (348 × 452 mm) at 14 HPI.

To appreciate the detail of his face, look at the large-scale head. Both heads have been charted at this scale so you can make a pair of pictures.

These charts are approximately 84 stitches wide by 96 stitches tall, and 110 by 102, about 6 × 6.9 inches (152 × 175 mm) and 7.9 × 7.3 inches (200 × 185 mm) on 14 HPI.

Piece stitched by Donna Harris

This small Super Robo was used in Chapter Two. You could also use the large Super Robo's head and breastplate separately for smaller projects.

These charts are approximately 68 stitches wide by 93 stitches tall, about 4.9 × 6.6 inches (124 × 168 mm) at 14 HPI.

Piece stitched by Carol Farmer

We've already seen Retro Robo in Chapter Two. He's typical of some of the earliest robot designs in anime and manga. Here he's stitched in whole stitches.

The robots have their own graphic sound effects, each charted in two sizes. *Gaooo* (in yellow) usually represents a drawn-out metallic clang or reverberation. *Go-o-n* (in red) also represents a clanging sound, often used for retro-styled robots.

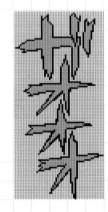

This chart is approximately 188 stitches wide by 166 stitches tall, about 13.4 × 11.8 inches (340 × 300 mm) at 14 HPI.

Piece stitched by Caroline McFadden and Michelle Easters

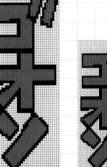  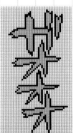

The smaller charts are approximately 36 stitches wide by 84 stitches tall, about 2.6 × 6 inches (66 × 152 mm) at 14 HPI. The larger charts are approximately 55 by 125 stitches, about 3.9 × 8.9 inches (99 × 226 mm) at 14 HPI.

ACTION MANGA PAGES
> USING THE CHARTS

IN CHAPTERS ONE and Two we built manga pages using robots and backgrounds. Following the same principles, choosing key images and placing other elements to harmonize with them, I've used two giant robots, two sound effects, and the downtown street background to make a big color picture in whole stitches.

First, I copied the street chart. The roadway had to be deeper to give the robots enough space to stand in front of the buildings, so I used the Change Design Area option in the Edit menu, adding plenty of extra depth, and colored the extra space to match the adjoining area. You can change the size again later if you add more than you need.

Next I pasted in the full-size Retro Robo and Super Robo charts, trying out different arrangements using Paste and Undo.

To make the robots stand out, I wanted a slightly simpler background, so I deleted some signs, filled in gaps, and made the windows gray. A taller building at one end of the chart fills the space and balances Super Robo's upraised fist. I added sound effects from the previous page, and changed the robots' colors using the Palette menu to add and replace threads.

This chart is approximately 350 stitches wide by 302 stitches tall. At 14 HPI it will measure about 25 × 21.6 inches (635 × 549 mm).

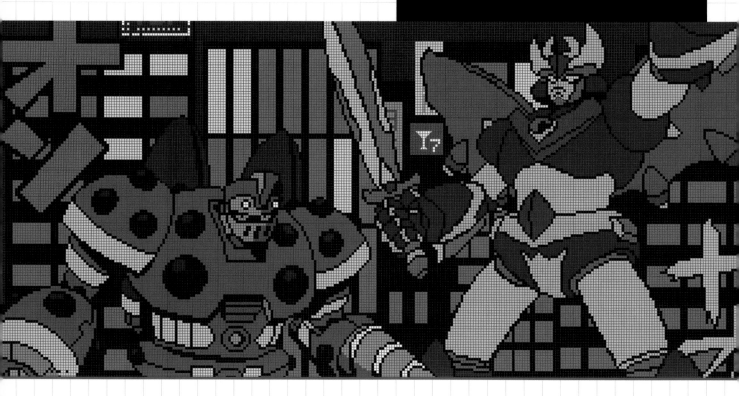

Colored fabric is a little more expensive than white or natural, but, if you don't want the effect of a fully stitched background, it will save you time and money. For this project, working on dark blue fabric saves 12 skeins of thread, almost 25,000 stitches, and many hours of work.

The next chapters suggest other ways to enhance your compositions. Chapter Five looks at screentone, texture, speedlines, and facial expressions. Chapter Six has English and Japanese lettering to show you how to make your own sound effects, headings, and dialogue.

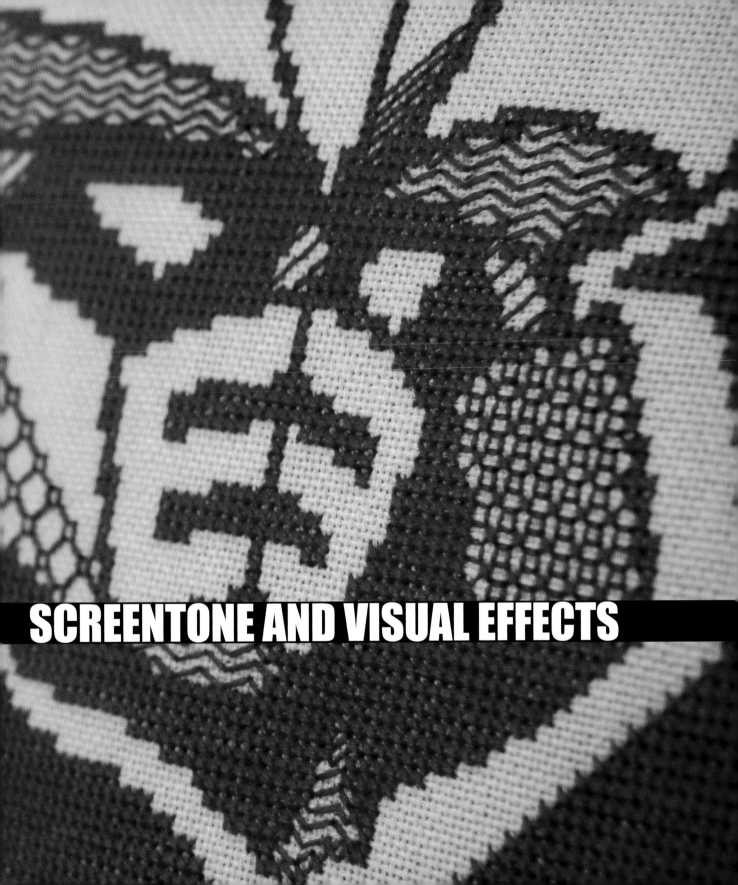

SCREENTONE AND VISUAL EFFECTS

ADDING DRAMA
>TEXTURE AND TONE

THE BACKGROUND DETAILS, highlights, and textures you choose for your image can add an extra dimension. A simple figure looks great on a plain background, but adding a few speedlines can give it the aura of movement. Putting a patch of texture in a background or on a costume creates the impression of greater detail, and can suggest a setting or story. Put bamboo behind the character's head to suggest a forest, or a cascade of stars or flowers to add a touch of romance.

All manga and anime images are outlined, but the lines vary from hair-fine to thick and blocky. A Japanese dip pen or brush makes powerful lines, the varied thickness making them very expressive. It's much more difficult to get this spontaneity in stitches—you need to consider whether to use whole stitch only, fractionals, or backstitch, and how thick the threads need to be to get the effect you want.

Screentone is a way of filling space, adding texture, and shading. Sheets of rub-down transfer paper come in many patterns that can be used for screentones. They can add detail to a background, indicate a setting, or just fill an area with abstract decoration. You can even download screentones to use on the computer.

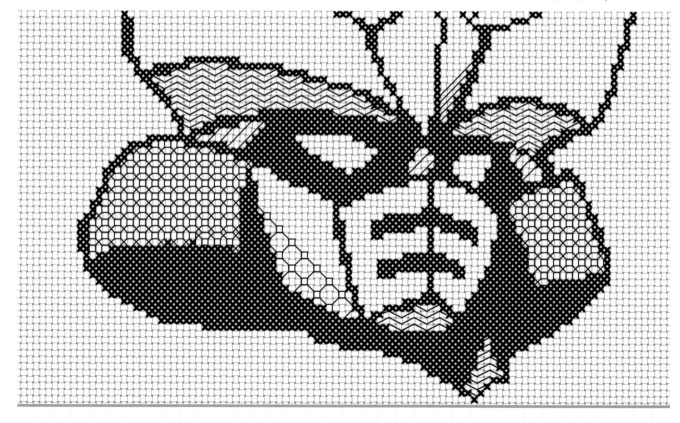

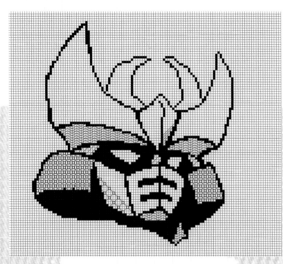

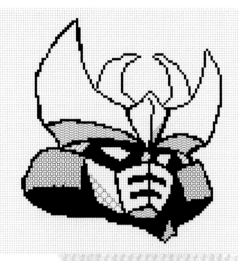

My "stitched screentones" are small, repeating patterns in straight stitch, backstitch, or double running stitch. The technique comes from blackwork, an ancient embroidery style brought to England by Henry VIII's Spanish queen, Catherine of Aragon. You can see how well stitched screentones work in this panel showing a robot head. By using dense stitching for areas of deep shadow, and lighter stitching for lighter areas, you can create form and texture.

By incorporating tones, textures, and speedlines as you plan your image, you can make it unique and give it your own personal style.

This chart is approximately 89 stitches wide by 95 stitches tall. At 14 HPI it will measure about 6.4 × 6.8 inches (163 × 173 mm).

Piece stitched by Chennell Hinton

ADDING DRAMA
> SPEEDLINES

SPEEDLINES FOLLOW THE shape of a movement. A straight movement generates straight lines—a swishing sword or a waving hand needs curved lines.

There are several ways to use speedlines. You might just want one or two to emphasize a particular movement, like the wagging of the dog's tail in this cute image.

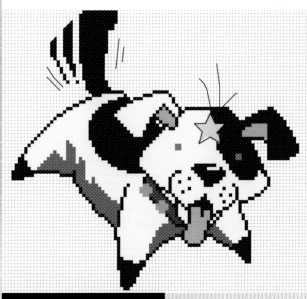

Look at the movement of the fist in this portrait of a boy robot. The upper lines are rough and strong, following the curve of the fist as it swings. The lower lines emphasize the movement of the arm but also help to define the area of the image, cutting off the rest of the robot's body to focus on the head and the flying fist.

This chart is approximately 90 stitches wide by 91 stitches tall, about 6.4 × 6.5 inches (163 × 165 mm) at 14 HPI.

Piece stitched by Nikki Thompson

The heaviest speedlines, near the tail, are in whole stitch, and the smaller ones are in backstitch. The blockiness of the heavy lines would overwhelm a more delicate image, yet without the finer backstitch lines they wouldn't have the same degree of animation.

This chart is approximately 73 stitches wide by 88 stitches tall. At 14 HPI it will measure about 5.2 × 6.3 inches (132 × 160 mm).

Piece stitched by Katie Oakley

For small lines, the thickness can be uniform, but for longer lines the thickest end, and greatest spread between lines, is farthest from where the movement starts. The tip of the dog's tail, opposite page, is moving fastest, so the lines echo the shape of the tail but are farther apart near the tip than at the base.

Design your image first, then add speedlines where they look most effective. There are a few examples of backstitch and whole stitch speedlines on the CD, but drawing your own for each project will give your work more spontaneity.

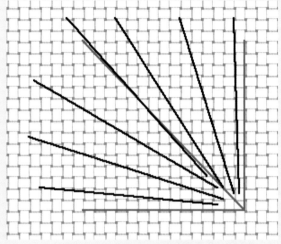

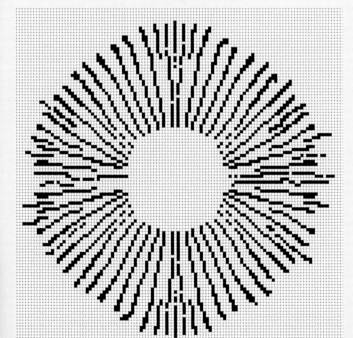

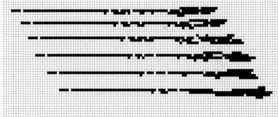

Putting speedlines with every movement will dilute their impact—save them for those you really want to emphasize.

TONE CHARTS
> SCREENTONES AND SPECKLES

YOU DON'T NEED screentones for full-color, anime-style images because color does the job of adding volume and depth. For monotone images, however, they can be very useful.

Look at the precise stitched patterns on this screentone sampler. Each consists of straight stitches, worked over two threads or one block of Aida. You can use backstitch or Holbein stitch. The left-hand side of the chart has more open patterns, with denser ones on the right, and mid-tone patterns down the center. This is a challenging sampler, even for an experienced stitcher.

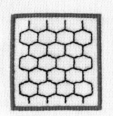
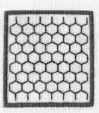
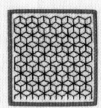

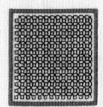
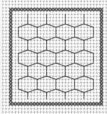
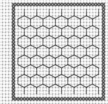
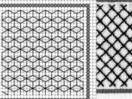

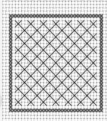
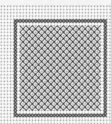

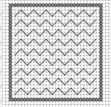

This chart is approximately 104 stitches wide by 141 stitches tall, about 7.4 × 10.1 inches (188 × 257 mm) at 14 HPI.

Piece stitched by Melusine Grey

There are the tones on the CD, but you can also make your own by combining them to create new patterns. If you look closely, you'll see that some of the patterns have been made by overlaying the center pattern on itself at a slightly offset angle.

Manga artists often put layers of tones on top of each other, scraping off one layer or more to create shadows and highlights. You can do the same thing in reverse, building up layers of denser tones around the lightest area. Here are two examples of this process.

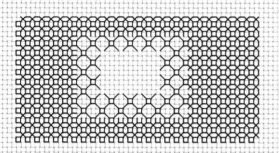 

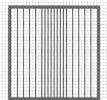  

 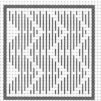 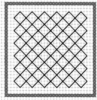

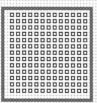 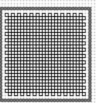

To use the tones in your own charts, just cut and paste them from the chart on the CD in small sections, taking care to line up each section so it fits with the others, until the area you want to cover with tone is filled in. Most stitchers like to do backstitch after all the other stitches in a project are finished. This is a good idea, as you'll see exactly where your screen-tone stitching needs to fit.

Keep the use of tone and shading very bold, and don't use so much that your image gets swamped with too much detail.

TONE CHARTS
> GRADATIONS AND SPECIAL BACKGROUNDS

IF YOU DON'T want to use stitched screentones, distinct tones of black and gray provide very effective volume and definition. On this page, black, white, and two tones of gray are used on a dark background to create the shading.

The modeling is bold, with small areas of detail around the eye and the ear. The gloved hand, turning up the collar, is just an outline.

This chart is approximately 154 stitches wide by 182 stitches tall. At 14 HPI it will measure about 11 × 13 inches (280 × 330 mm).

Piece stitched by Malin Stegman McCallion

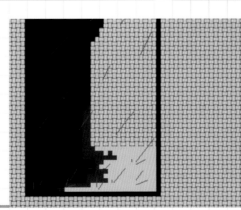

In the small panel, the man's shape is only roughly suggested. The rain is indicated with lines of blue. Notice how small, angled stitches suggest heavy rain hitting the pavement and bouncing back.

Screentones can also be used to create backgrounds—regardless of whether you want a tiled roof, stone wall, bamboo grove, or even an entire street.

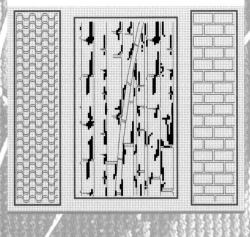

In the Ronin image in Chapter Four, one variation shows thick bamboo stems behind the character's head, taken from a chart on the CD featuring basic background elements. They're all worked in backstitch or Holbein stitch. The bamboo charts use whole stitches for texture and fractionals for the leaves.

The amounts of thread and fabric you need for adding backgrounds and shading will depend on the size of the area you stitch. Check the key for your finished chart.

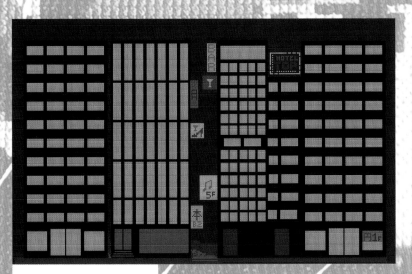

The color chart is approximately 350 stitches wide by 238 stitches tall. At 14 HPI it will measure about 25 × 17 inches (635 × 432 mm).

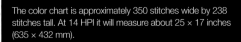

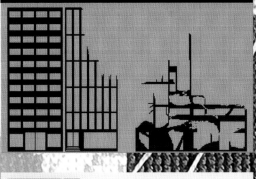

There's a chart for a nighttime downtown street on the CD. It's in color, but you can change the lit windows, painted doorways, and colorful neon for white or gray. If you want to make the buildings and sky white, outline the buildings, windows, and doors in backstitch so they don't disappear. There's also a devastated version of the same street in just black and white.

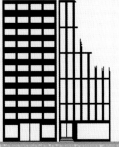

EFFECTS CHARTS
> COMEDY

FACIAL EXPRESSION IS vital to comedy, and eyes are the most visible feature of the manga face. They signal key emotions, and it's crucial to get the look of the eyes right to get your message across. The rest of the face, although often very simply drawn, is just as important.

The CD has a chart with different facial expressions and face shapes so you can try designing your own. Draw the expression before you add the hair. Once you've got the face as you want it, add hair to suit.

It's possible to make expressive eyes and faces without working backstitch—there are several examples in this book and on the CD—but it's difficult to get any strong emotional impact without it, especially on smaller images. Unless you're prepared to spend time on backstitch that details eyes (and other facial features) in your projects, you'll lose out on intensity. The placement of each stitch gives expression to the face you're creating.

This chart is approximately 120 stitches wide by 140 stitches tall. At 14 HPI it will measure about 8.6 × 10 inches (218 × 254 mm).

Piece stitched by Helen McCarthy

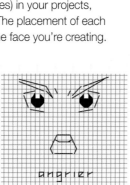

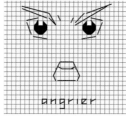

Here's a page using changes of expression and strong color to make a dynamic image. As the character's rage mounts, his eyebrows pull closer together, his eyes narrow, and his face distorts. The little fangs in his mouth, and the hair standing on end, show he's completely lost control by the time we reach the last panel.

Each image is only partly framed and overlaps the next, giving the impression of escalating tension as the panels tumble down the page. The edges of the last one are exploding outward.

The lettering supports the images. A simple, blocky style in the first panel is calm but forceful. The emphatic "NOT" in panel two doesn't overwhelm the scratchier lettering in the final panel because of the red capitals and exclamation marks.

EFFECTS CHARTS
> DRAMA

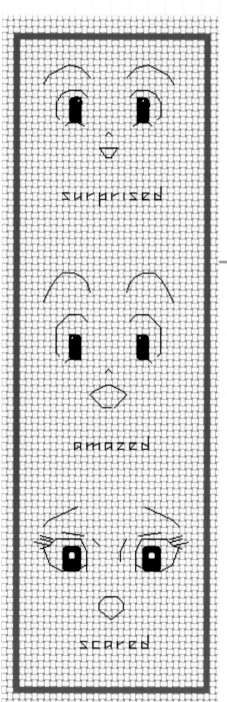

Facial expression is vital for drama, too. These three sketches, in backstitch with the pupils defined in cross-stitch, show the shift from surprise to horror.

First, the nose is slightly upturned and the cheeks have moved upward as the smile starts. Then the eyebrows go higher, the eyes and mouth are wider, but the cheeks are still curving upward and the upturned nose is still visible. Finally, the eyes are wide, with lines around them. Their highlights are bigger and lower. The mouth is wide but pinched, in a gasp rather than a smile, and the nose has vanished. The eyebrows are higher in the middle but the sides are pulled down, giving the face an anxious look.

Notice the different highlights in the eyes. On the frightened face, they can be bigger because the whole pupil is bigger.

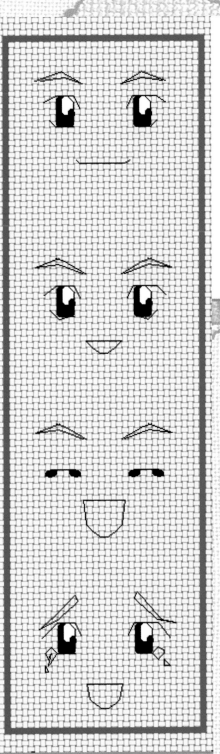

Now look at these four stages of happiness. The mouth is wide and curved up at the corners to show a good mood. This is a guy—a feminine mouth would be smaller, about half the width in relation to the eyes, and the eyebrows would be smoother and finer. In the second frame he's even happier—his eyes are wider, his eyebrows and his cheeks have moved slightly up, and his mouth is slightly open.

The third image shows him laughing. His eyebrows are higher, his eyes almost vanish, and his mouth is wide open, so his chin looks smaller. In the last frame he's crying with happiness, and embarrassed to be so overcome with emotion—his eyebrows have moved down at the outer corners as he narrows his eyes slightly to stem the tears flowing from them, and his mouth has moved slightly upward as he tries to control his wobbling lower lip.

When absolutely overcome with emotion, the mouth opens wide, showing a line of teeth, and the chin vanishes. Eyes become tiny slits with tears shooting out, and lines form between the eyebrows as the face crumples with emotion.

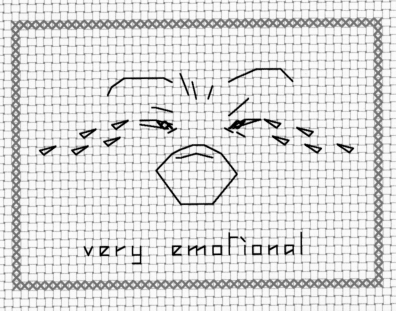

very emotional

YAMA
MOUNTAIN

A
FIRE

LETTERING

ADDING IMPACT
> JAPANESE LETTERING

JAPANESE WRITING IS very complex. Instead of combining letters into different words, the Japanese make up words from symbols representing sounds. They use three different scripts to write.

They began to evolve this writing in the fourth century AD, adapting Chinese symbols and calling them kanji. They also made two Japanese script systems, katakana and hiragana, known together as kana.

Katakana is an angular script designed for easy writing. Katakana characters are used in telegrams, for words borrowed from other languages (such as terebi and anime), and foreign names. Japanese has no upper case, so katakana are used for emphasis as well as for onomatopoeic words, like sound effects in manga. Katakana is also used to write Ainu, Northern Japan's aboriginal language.

Hiragana is a beautiful, flowing script, which is also easy to learn. Children learn kana in elementary school but don't begin to study kanji until much later. Nowadays hiragana is used for word endings and parts of speech, for words where the kanji are very complex or obsolete, and for school textbooks, children's literature, and comics.

Japanese is written in columns, top to bottom and right to left. But mobile phones and email are changing the way Japanese is written—people are starting to write left to right across the page. You're an artist, not a linguist, so arrange characters in whatever way suits your project.

Look at this small sampler, stitched on 14-count Aida, using just two colors. The two characters of the word manga are arranged one above the other, with the English word below. The blue letters are a more standardized type, but the red ones are looser and bolder, resembling Japanese calligraphy.

This image is approximately 72 stitches wide by 107 stitches tall, about 5.1 × 7.6 inches (130 × 193 mm) at 14 HPI.

Piece stitched by Beverley Shaw

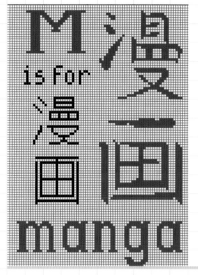

Stitched here is the Japanese character for love, *ai*. These designs are ideal for wall hangings, book covers, or greeting cards.

This image is approximately 46 stitches wide by 90 stitches tall, about 3.3 × 6.4 inches (84 × 163 mm) at 14 HPI.

Piece stitched by Rhianydd Summerset

SAMPLER
> KATAKANA

THIS SAMPLER shows the 46 basic syllables of katakana, with their English equivalents. Katakana was originally "men's script," evolved by Buddhist monks. Characters are grouped by sound. Each group has the same opening consonant followed by one of the five vowel sounds, in the order a-i-u-e-o.

Of course, there are more than 46 sounds in Japanese, so the basic characters are modified with diacritical marks—small symbols placed at the upper right-hand corner of the character—or by combinations of characters. This table shows how diacritical marks and combined characters are used.

va	vi	vu	ve	vo
ヴァ	ヴィ	ヴ	ヴェ	ヴォ
wi	we	wo		
ヴィ	ヴェ	ウォ		
fa	fi	fe	fo	
ファ	フィ	フェ	フォ	
ti	tu			
ティ	トゥ			
di	du			
ディ	ドゥ			
she				
シェ				
je				
ジェ				
che				
チェ				

ga	gi	gu	ge	go
ガ	ギ	グ	ゲ	ゴ
za	ji	zu	ze	zo
ザ	ジ	ズ	ゼ	ゾ
da	ji	zu	de	do
ダ	ヂ	ヅ	デ	ド
ba	bi	bu	be	bo
バ	ビ	ブ	ベ	ボ
pa	pi	pu	pe	po
パ	ピ	プ	ペ	ポ

ア A	イ I	ウ U	エ E	オ O
カ KA	キ KI	ク KU	ケ KE	コ KO
サ SA	シ SHI	ス SU	セ SE	ソ SO
タ TA	チ CHI	ツ TSU	テ TE	ト TO
ナ NA	ニ NI	ヌ NU	ネ NE	ノ NO
ハ HA	ヒ HI	フ FU	ヘ HE	ホ HO
マ MA	ミ MI	ム MU	メ ME	モ MO
ヤ YA		ユ YU		ヨ YO
ラ RA	リ RI	ル RU	レ RE	ロ RO
ワ WA		ヲ WO		ン N

KATAKANA

This sampler is approximately 144 stitches wide by 280 stitches tall. At 14 HPI it measures about 10.3 × 20 inches (262 × 508 mm).

Piece stitched by Paula Taylor

KATAKANA

The bamboo frame sets off the rich gold and garnet-red lettering. It's a large piece, and the main challenge is keeping the borders neat and making sure the characters are arranged in straight lines.

The katakana sampler would be a lovely housewarming gift for a contemporary home, and its simplicity will appeal to both men and women. It could also make a classic birth sampler for parents who don't care for fluffy animals or Victoriana. You can replace the lettering at the bottom of the frame with the baby's name and date of birth, or, using the full version of the software on the CD, extend the frame and make room for the lettering above or below the characters inside it.

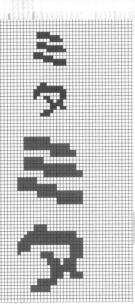

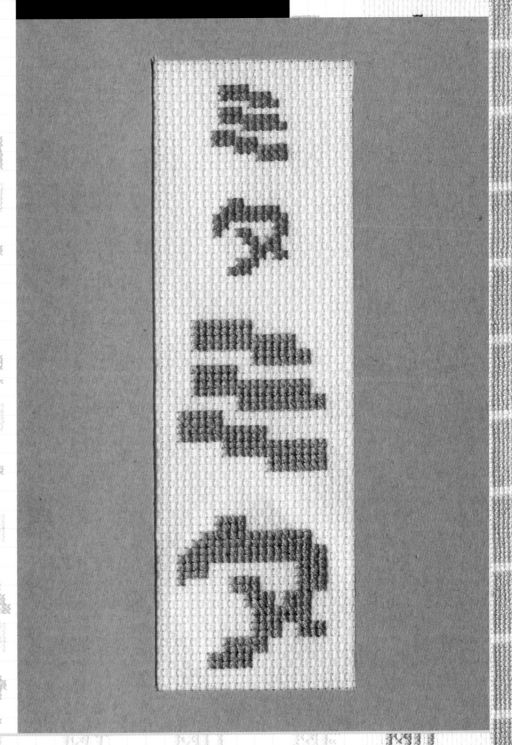

The enlarged characters are each approximately 20 stitches square, about 1.4 inches square (36 mm sq) at 14 HPI.

Piece stitched by Nikki Thompson

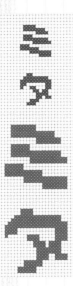

Since katakana is used for foreign names, the individual characters make unusual small monograms for table linen or towels. For instance, for a couple named Michael and Taylor, take the characters Mi and Ta, arranged either traditionally one above the other, or side by side.

The small chart shows these two katakana characters, at the same scale as in the sampler but enlarged by converting each single stitch into a square of four stitches. This keeps the exact proportions of the character, but makes it twice as big.

SAMPLER
> HIRAGANA

THIS SAMPLER SETS out the basic syllables of modern hiragana script, laid out in the same style as the katakana sampler on page 110.

ga	gi	gu	ge	go
が	ギ	ぐ	げ	ご
za	**ji**	**zu**	**ze**	**zo**
ざ	じ	ず	ぜ	ぞ
da	**ji**	**zu**	**de**	**do**
だ	ぢ	づ	で	ど
ba	**bi**	**bu**	**be**	**bo**
は	び	ぶ	べ	ば
pa	**pi**	**pu**	**pe**	**po**
ぱ	ぴ	ぷ	ぺ	ぱ

kya	キャ	kyu	キゅ	kyo	キョ
sha	しゃ	shu	しゅ	sho	しょ
cha	さゃ	chu	さゅ	cho	さょ
nya	にゃ	nyu	にゅ	nyo	にょ
hya	ひゃ	hyu	ひゅ	hyo	ひょ
mya	ムゃ	myu	ムゅ	myo	ムょ
rya	りゃ	ryu	りゅ	ryo	りょ
gya	ギゃ	gyu	ギゅ	gyo	ギょ
ja	じゃ	ju	じゅ	jo	じょ
bya	びゃ	byu	びゅ	byo	びょ
pya	ぴゃ	pyu	ぴゅ	pyo	ぴょ

Hiragana uses the same method of combining characters and diacritical marks to represent more sounds, as shown in this table.

Designed to complement the katakana sampler, this piece relies on the use of rich, yet restrained, color and regular spacing for its impact. Since hiragana was originally "women's script," used by female writers and poets, this would make an ideal birth or graduation sampler for a girl. Like the katakana chart, it will probably take around 30 hours to stitch.

Regular size and arrangement is a very important feature of Japanese script. Where Western children write in ruled notebooks, Japanese children have notebooks ruled in squares, with each character fitting into one square. The order of the strokes with which the character is written is also important.

In designing these characters, the main challenge was simplifying the flowing shapes without losing the overall outline. If you enlarge them for your own projects, be careful that you keep the character legible—distortion can work for sound effects and logos, but it's pointless if it obscures your message. The best way to be sure of keeping the character correct is to look at a book on writing kana, or to log onto one of the many websites that have kana charts.

This chart is approximately 144 stitches wide by 280 stitches tall. At 14 HPI it will measure about 10.3 × 20 inches (262 × 508 mm).

Piece stitched by Laura Riley

You could use single characters or groups of characters for small projects like greetings cards, nameplates, or bookmarks. This chart shows the hiragana for *omedeto*—congratulations—worked in bright colors, suitable for a birthday card or new baby congratulations card.

This chart is approximately 52 stitches wide by 18 stitches tall, about 3.7 × 1.3 inches (94 × 33 mm) at 14 HPI.

Piece stitched by Nikki Thompson

SAMPLER
> SOUND EFFECTS

JAPANESE SOUND EFFECTS—or gitaigo—are looked at briefly in Chapter Two, on pages 50–51. These samplers demonstrate how the characters can be used to make beautiful designs.

This small sampler, showing a few sound effects, was stitched using both katakana and hiragana. A powerful *ban*—a big impact or explosion—dominates the image, and quieter sounds are arranged around it. You'll find more Japanese sound effects on the CD, and here's a list of some to try charting for yourself in kana.

This chart is approximately 60 stitches wide by 110 stitches tall. At 14 HPI it will measure about 4.3 × 7.9 inches (109 × 201 mm).

Piece stitched by Carol Farmer

JAPANESE SOUND EFFECTS

BAN – big impact or explosion, like BANG!

BARA BARA – rattle

BARI BARI – crunch, as when eating crisp foods, or loud scratching sounds

BASA – rustle, like cloth or paper sliding

CHUU – squeak (mouse, small animal, or tiny child)

DAN – knock

DOKIDOKI – rapid heartbeat

DOKIN, DOKUN – heart thumping

DON – gunshot or explosion

DORON, DORONPAPA – sound of a magical transformation

GOOOO – sound of flames

KACHA – click

KIRAKIRA – sparkle

NYAN – meow

PACHI – a sharp, snapping sound like a click, crack, crackle, or handclap

PARIPARI – crackle of energy or electricity

PIN PON – ding dong

PIYO – peep or cheep

POCHIPOCHI – regular noise, like water dripping or popping bubble wrap

SAAA, ZAAA – sound of wind or rain, the ocean, rustling wind in leaves

SHAAA – swish, something slicing through the air, like a sword

SHIIN – complete silence

UUUUU – whooo, either whistling wind or noise from a jubilant/rowdy crowd

WAA – crowd noise

WANWAN – woof woof

Remember that you can write your sound effects in any language—it doesn't have to be Japanese to look good. Japanese lettering is beautiful in its own right, so don't just consider it as caption fodder. Use it for samplers, images, and pictures where its beauty can be appreciated.

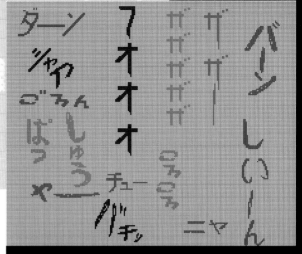

This chart is approximately 206 stitches wide by 283 stitches tall. At 14 HPI it will measure about 14.7 × 20.2 inches (373 × 513 mm).

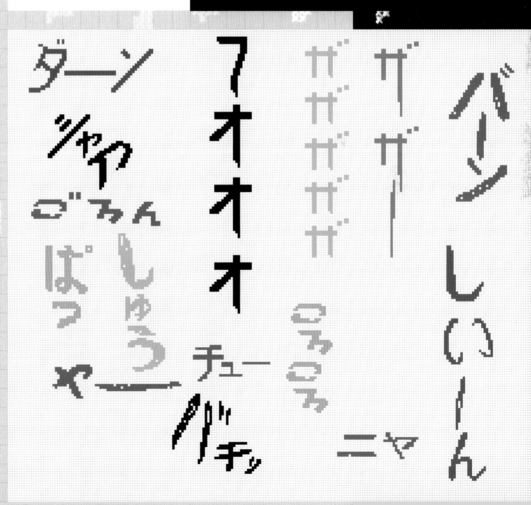

SAMPLER
> KANJI

IN WRITTEN JAPANESE there are 1,945 kanji in everyday use, and thousands that are rarely used. Each can be read in a number of different ways, depending on the context. Their outlines make wonderful designs. If you can't find anything suitable in these charts, consult a book or website.

The miniature sampler, stitched in dark blue on a red linen band, shows kanji for the numbers from one to ten. You could finish this in a few hours.

The chart is approximately 45 stitches wide by 77 stitches tall. At 14 HPI it will measure about 3.2 × 5.5 inches (81 × 140 mm).

Piece stitched by Vicky Downing

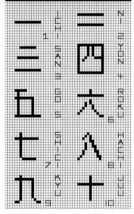

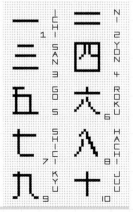

Many characters are based on ancient drawings of the object they represent. This is still obvious in "mountain" and "river." These beautiful characters are stitched on a two-tone background that echoes their meaning, with the main Japanese readings alongside the character and the English description below.

The charts are approximately 68 stitches wide by 73 stitches tall and 71 by 58. At 14 HPI they will measure about 4.9 × 5.2 inches (124 × 132 mm) and 5.1 × 4.1 inches (130 × 104 mm).

Piece stitched by Caroline McFadden

JITSU NICHI SUN DAY	日
HON MOTO BOOK MAIN	本
DEN TA RICEFIELD	田
MAN MIGARINI INVOLUNTARILY	漫
GA KAKU PICTURE	画
SEN KAWA RIVER	川
SAN YAMA MOUNTAIN	山
SUI MIZU WATER	水
KA HI FIRE	火
TAI DAI BIG	大
SHO CHIISAI SMALL	小
DAN OTOKO MAN	男
JO ONNA WOMAN	女
AI ITO LOVE AFFECTION	愛
HYAKU HUNDRED	百
SEN CHI THOUSAND	千
EN MARU YEN ROUND	円

Other characters are less recognizable to modern readers. These two, "sun" and "fire," were again stitched with backgrounds emphasizing their meaning.

The card has the characters for man, woman, and *yen*—Japanese for money. It would make a humorous wedding greeting, taking very little time. The characters are taken from the kanji scroll sampler, which could be used as a wall hanging or bell pull, or to make borders for towels, or table or bed linen.

This chart is approximately 64 stitches wide by 269 stitches tall, about 4.6 × 19.2 inches (117 × 488 mm) at 14 HPI.

The charts are approximately 64 stitches wide by 63 stitches tall and 67 by 68. At 14 HPI they will measure about 4.6 × 4.5 inches (117 × 114 mm) and 4.8 × 4.9 inches (122 × 124 mm).

Piece stitched by Dishani Biyanwila

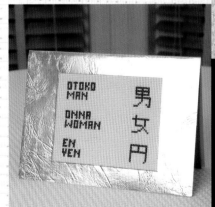

This chart is approximately 56 stitches wide by 47 stitches tall. At 14 HPI it will measure about 4 × 3.4 inches (102 × 86 mm).

Piece stitched by Nikki Thompson

SAMPLER
> WESTERN LETTERING

THESE SAMPLERS HAVE a range of lettering that you can use for captions, headings, and dedications, including some smaller ones suitable for word balloons or narrative panels. You've seen some of them used in various projects in this book.

The decorative borders and emblems can also be used for other projects. This small sampler was stitched with *mon*—ancient family crests. The borders are variations on a traditional Japanese arrowhead design, found in textiles and art since the early medieval period. It needs to be worked with precision for maximum impact.

The chart is approximately 76 stitches wide by 110 stitches tall, about 5.4 × 7.9 inches (137 × 201 mm) at 14 HPI.

Piece stitched by Lisa Brown

The borders of the two larger charts use similar patterns, which can be used to fill in backgrounds or make patterns on belts, sashes, and other items of clothing.

The charts are approximately 150 stitches wide by 222 stitches tall, and 150 by 130, about 10.7 × 15.9 inches (272 × 404 mm) or 10.7 × 9.3 inches (272 × 236 mm) at 14 HPI.

The Dash alphabet began as a heading for the Super Robo manga page in Chapter Two. The style was so much fun, that I have charted the alphabet in two different sizes.

The small chart is approximately 106 stitches wide by 70 stitches tall. At 14 HPI it will measure about 7.6 × 5 inches (193 × 127 mm).

The medium chart is approximately 151 stitches wide by 99 stitches tall. At 14 HPI it will measure around 10.8 by 7.1 inches (274 × 180 mm).

The script heading on the Rain Boy page in Chapter Two is quite ornate and feminine, but it's a variation of Dash. It's a lot of fun to vary alphabets, but keep checking the original as you work to make sure you keep the proportions right.

Remember that you can enlarge any whole stitch alphabet simply by charting four stitches for every one on the original chart.

REFERENCE

USEFUL RESOURCES
> BIBLIOGRAPHY AND GLOSSARY

ALLEN, Jeanne:
Designer's Guide to Japanese Stencil Patterns 2,
pub. Chronicle Books, 1988,
ISBN 978 0877015499
An excellent record of traditional stencil patterns.

BOUQUILLARD, Jocelyn, and Marquet, Christopher:
Hokusai, First Manga Master,
pub. Abrams, 2007,
ISBN 978 0810993419

BROPHY, Philip: Tezuka: The Marvel of Manga,
exhibition catalog, pub. National Gallery of Victoria,
2006, ISBN 978 0724102785
Packed with inspiring images by the "god of manga."

CLEMENTS, Jonathan, and McCarthy, Helen:
The Anime Encyclopedia: Japanese Animation since 1917,
pub. (US) Stone Bridge Press, 2nd edition, 2006,
ISBN 978 1933330105;
pub. (UK) Titan Books, ISBN 978 1845765002
The most complete book on anime in English, with superb
Steve Kyte artwork.

DILLMONT, Therese de:
The Complete Encyclopedia of Needlework,
pub. Running Press, 2002,
ISBN 978 0762413188
One of the best books on the subject, covering every kind of hand
needlecraft, constantly in print since 1884.

GRAVETT, Paul: Manga: Sixty Years of Japanese Comics,
pub. (US) Collins Design; pub. (UK) Laurence King, 2004,
ISBN 978 1856693912
By a well-known British comic expert, packed with pictures.

HARLOW, Eve:
The New Anchor Book of Canvaswork Stitches and Patterns,
pub. David & Charles, 1989,
ISBN 978 0715391860
A mine of ideas, with adaptable stitches for different fabrics.

LEWIS, Bruce:
Draw Manga—How to Draw Manga In Your Own Unique Style,
pub. Anova Books/Collins & Brown, 2005,
ISBN 978 1843401889
An inspirational reference book by leading U.S. manga artist.

McCARTHY, Helen:
500 Essential Anime Movies,
pub. Ilex Press, 2008, ISBN 978 1905814282
Anime available in English, with color pictures to inspire you.

MITAMURA, Yasuko K.:
Let's Learn Hiragana,
pub. Kodansha International, 1985,
ISBN 978 0870117091
Let's Learn Katakana,
ISBN 978 0870117190
Learn to read and write kana—easy and fun.

SCHODT, Frederik L.:
Manga! Manga! The World of Japanese Comics,
pub. Kodansha International, 1986,
ISBN 978 0870117527
Great English-language introduction to Japanese comics,
by a renowned translator and interpreter—packed with pictures.

SCOTT BARON, Hayden, and Sweatdrop Studios:
500 Manga Characters,
pub. Ilex Press, 2007,
ISBN 978 1905814039
High-resolution, copyright-free images on CD-ROM,
ready to load onto computer and use in your own designs.

STUDIO, Yishan:
500 Manga Creatures,
pub. Ilex Press, 2008, ISBN 978 1905814305
As *500 Manga Characters* but with creatures.

USEFUL WEBSITES
http://stitchdirect.co.uk/forum/
Lively stitchers' forum and place to buy stitching materials.
http://cross-stitching.infopop.cc/eve
The website of a well-known stable of British stitch magazines.
Charts, mail order, and a stitchers' forum.
http://www.acrosstownstitching.co.uk
Stitching supplies—great service, fast delivery, and good prices.
http://www.animenewsnetwork.com/
English-language news and information on anime.
http://comipress.com
English-language news and information on manga.
http://www.kanjisite.com
All about kanji—read, write, and learn onsite.

Aida (say ay-ee-da or ayda) Fabric for cross-stitch that has threads grouped in blocks to make stitching easier. Available in different stitch counts/HPI.

Anime (say ah nee may) Japanese word for animation.

Binca Six HPI version of Aida often used for teaching children to stitch.

-chan Suffix added to a name, usually translated as darling; used for small children, younger female relatives, or by a boyfriend/husband for his beloved. Sometimes considered patronizing for adults, but mostly accepted for children.

Chara Short for character.

Chart A diagram with symbols, color blocks, or both, showing where to make each stitch to create a counted-thread embroidery.

Chibi Japanese word meaning small. Sometimes abbreviated to CB.

Counted-thread embroidery Embroidery worked from charts or designs by counting the threads of the base fabric to determine the position of each stitch.

Cross-stitch A form of counted-thread embroidery made up of crossed stitches. Can also be worked without counting, using designs stamped onto fabric.

Embroidery hoop or frame A wooden or plastic frame to keep fabric rigid while stitching.

Evenweave Fabric with an even number of horizontal and vertical threads per inch, used for counted-thread embroidery and cross-stitch. It can be woven from natural or man-made fibers.

Floss Another name for stranded cotton.

Frame A wooden, plastic, or other surround for displaying an image.

Hanging A textile or embroidery displayed hanging from a rigid bar, with no frame or mount.

Hannya A character and type of mask used in classical Japanese theater, representing a beautiful woman transformed into a monster by jealousy over her unrequited love.

Hiragana One of the two kana script systems used to write Japanese. Originally used by women.

HPI—Holes Per Inch The number of holes in a linear inch of fabric, used to describe Aida or Binca.

Kana The collective name for the two native Japanese script systems, katakana and hiragana.

Kanji Japanese name for the characters used to write Japanese words, originally adopted from China.

Katakana One of the two kana script systems used to write Japanese. Originally used by men.

Kawaii Japanese word meaning cute.

Kimono Japanese word for a garment, used for the outer robe but also the entire outfit.

Manga Japanese word for comics, though "comics" is also used.

Mangaka Japanese word for someone who creates original manga.

Mecha An abbreviation of "mechanism" or "mechanical," used to describe any machine but particularly robots.

Mon A Japanese family crest, often displayed in a circle or roundel on garments, flags, and weapons.

Mount A card or fabric surround that borders an image within, or instead of, a frame.

Mount board, mounting board A rigid backing board on which needlework is fixed to keep it straight.

Oni Japanese demon.

Ronin A masterless samurai, usually a wanderer or mercenary.

Samurai Warriors originating in medieval Japan.

Stitch count The number of stitches in a linear inch of evenweave fabric. (See also thread count and HPI.)

Stranded cotton The thread most often used for cross-stitch, sold in skeins of six-stranded thread to be divided up as required. Also known as floss.

Tankobon A paperback volume collecting episodes of a popular manga serial, usually printed on better quality paper with some color pages.

Thread count The number of threads in a linear inch of evenweave fabric. This is not necessarily the same as the stitch count. For example, stitching over two threads of fabric with a thread count of 28 (28 threads per inch) gives a stitch count of 14 stitches per inch, but the fabric has a thread count of 28, which can also be described as 28 HPI (holes per inch).

CHART INDEX
> CHARTS BY PAGE NUMBER

CHART INDEX

> CONTINUED

ACKNOWLEDGMENTS

Picture Credits:

Illustrations: p 6, Yishan Li; p 22–29, Axel Bernal.
Photographs: p 8, Jupiter Images; p 9, The Bridgeman Art Library/
Victoria & Albert Museum, London, UK; p 17, Stepan Popov;
p 23 & 27, Jamie Wilson.

Lifestyle photography: Rachel Day
Stitch photography: Chris Gatcum

**Dedicated to the three women responsible for my needle addiction:
my grandmother, Ellen Kenny, my junior school teacher, Lilian Teresa
Bowditch, and my friend, Barbara Edwards.**

Thanks to everyone who has helped me with this book, including:
Steve Kyte, my favorite cross-stitch designer; The Manga Stitching Team,
credited alongside their work, all fantastic stitchers and fun to work with;
Barbara Edwards and Julie Tottey, inspiring crafters and great friends;
Louise Townend of Across Town Stitching, for fast delivery and superb
service; Tim Pilcher, for believing this book could work when other
commissioning editors just laughed themselves silly; The whole Ilex Press
team, especially Chris Gatcum, Nick Jones, and Ellie Wilson; Jeff Tullin of
Ursa Software for prompt and patient tech support; Delicate Stitches in
Kentish Town, London, my nearest stitch shop, whose huge range of stock
averted several crises; Les Meehan for excellent advice on photography;
Cross-Stitching.com and Cross Stitch Direct online forums; Frederik
L. Schodt, for helping the English-speaking world to appreciate manga.

Special thanks also to Tash Tori Arts & Crafts, in Lewes, UK.